America's Stamps

The Story of One Hundred Years
of U.S. Postage Stamps

"Neither snow nor rain nor heat nor gloom of night stays these couriers from the swift completion of their appointed rounds"

Herodotus

America's Stamps

The Story of One Hundred Years of U.S. Postage Stamps

Maud and Miska Petersham

The Macmillan Company
New York

The Philatelic Foundation has examined and read this book and finds its information accurate and considers it of considerable value in presenting the attractions of stamp collecting to those of all ages.

The Philatelic Foundation
ALFRED F. LICHTENSTEIN
Chairman, 1947

The Macmillan Company, New York
Collier-Macmillan Canada, Ltd., Toronto, Ontario
Printed in the United States of America

FIFTH PRINTING, 1967

CONTINENTAL POSTRIDER
1775   1789

THIS book pictures the United States stamps as they have been issued for over one hundred years. Stamps on letters carried by jolting stage-coaches, stamps on mail locked in the saddle pockets of the Pony Express rider, and stamps on letters bearing tragic messages from Civil War prison camps, down to the air mail stamps which carried letters to the homesick G.I. stationed in all parts of the world—these stamps are all here.

The book is not a stamp catalogue but a picture album of the United States. The little squares of gummed paper which have been issued for postage all these years, tell the story of the men who created the nation, and the adventures and the struggles of the young nation as it grew to be one of the greatest nations of the world.

This book also tells a little about the stamps themselves, and why and when they were issued.

In collecting the philatelic material we are deeply indebted to James Hoffman, without whose enthusiasm and interest the book might never have been completed. We acknowledge with appreciation the loan of valuable material and the checking of information by Frank W. Rosell, Sylvester Colby, Sidney F. Barrett, Robert A. Siegel, and Winthrop S. Boggs.

Maud and Miska Petersham

Contents

Issues Arranged Alphabetically

America's Stamps

The Story of One Hundred Years
of U.S. Postage Stamps

Stampless Covers

COFFEE HOUSE MAIL

The old sailing-ship captain with weather-beaten face left his ship and strode across the wharf of the port of Little New York. He was carrying a leather pouch filled with mail, and he made his way straight to the near-by Coffee House Tavern. Eager, anxious-eyed men and women had already crowded aboard his ship and claimed many of the letters he had brought on his long voyage.

In the tavern the captain carefully opened his sack and took out the letters which were folded sheets without envelopes, sealed with a round blob of red wax. He laid them on the table, where they would be held until called for. Then the old captain hung his pouch on a peg in the wall and left it there. On his return trip he would carry mail back to the port from which he had sailed. The fee was one English penny for a single-sheet letter, or twopence for a double-sheet.

In this way mail passed back and forth between the first American colonists and their friends and families far across the seas. A Coffee House Tavern or a specified house served as a post office. One of the first official references to the Post is in a law passed by the Massachusetts Bay Colony. In 1639 it was decreed "that notice be given that Richard Fairbanks, his house in Boston, is the place appointed for all letters, which are brought from beyond the Seas or are to bee sent thither." In Philadelphia it was at the sign of the "Death of the Fox" in Strawberry Alley that William Penn established a Post. The Coffee House Post was in existence as late as 1774.

Few letters passed between the lonely towns and scattered settlements of the early settlers. These were carried by a private messenger or a post-rider on horseback who, with letters safe in his saddlebag, forded the streams and followed the Indian trails through dense forests. He was warned not to "detayne, conceale or open any letters" on his journey. It was the Virginia law in 1657 that a planter must forfeit a hogshead of tobacco unless he furnish a rider to carry dispatches promptly from his plantation to the next.

As the Colonies grew and roads were built between the larger towns, mail was carried by creaking stagecoaches which jolted over the deep ruts or splashed through seas of mud. The postal service was slow, irregular, and costly.

Governor Lovelace of New York tried to establish a regular postrider service in 1672 and he decreed that a "post shall goe monthly between New York and Boston." This was the beginning of one of the earliest mail routes. The official Colonial Post started in 1691 with a grant from the English Crown to Thomas Neale, to establish a postal system within the Colonies. However, the operation of this service proved to be too costly and passed directly under the British Post.

The Colonies themselves did not take over the postal system until just before the American Revolution.

There were no stamps on our earliest colonial letters. At first there was nothing to show that a letter had passed through the Post.

As the Colonies grew, post offices were established and postmasters placed the words "Paid" or "Due" on the folded letter sheet. Envelopes were as yet but little used. Usually the postmaster added the amount, the date, and the name of the town in which the letter was posted. The general custom was to pay the fee when the letter was received. Colonial covers with their crude postmarks tell a story of small towns and settlements, many of which later became the great cities of today. The colonial postmarks are most interesting from a historical standpoint.

This is an old Penny Postman of Albany, New York, who delivered the mail brought there by stagecoach. The letters he delivered had postmarks similar to the ones pictured.

Postmasters' Provisional Stamps

Government postage stamps were not issued until about sixty-six years after the Colonies had won their independence and become the United States of America. For two years before the first issue of stamps, postmasters in several cities provided stamps themselves to indicate the prepayment of postage. This they did as a convenience to the public. On many of the Provisionals, as the postmaster stamps are called, the initials or the signature of the postmaster was added. Some Provisionals were adhesive stamps. Some were printed or hand-stamped on the envelope. The Postmasters' Provisional stamps are very rare and valuable. They were the forerunners of the regular United States postage stamps.

Examples of Postmasters' Provisionals

New York, N. Y.

Baltimore, Md.

Saint Louis, Mo.

New Haven, Conn.

The First Government Issue

*I*ssue of 1847

In 1847, after an Act of Congress authorized the use of adhesive stamps, the Post Office Department brought out two stamps, a 5 cent and a 10 cent denomination. Although adhesive stamps were already in use in Europe, this was our first government issue in the United States.

The 5 cent stamp was printed in a light brown color and carried a portrait of the first Postmaster General, Benjamin Franklin. Franklin had been Postmaster at Philadelphia and then had been appointed by the English Crown as Postmaster General of all the British Colonies in America. Later, when the Colonies themselves took over the postal system, Franklin was chosen their first Postmaster General. He opened new post roads, shortened the time required for transporting the mail, and did much more to improve the colonial postal service. His son William was a postrider about Philadelphia.

The 10 cent stamp, printed in black, bore a portrait of George Washington. After the Colonies had won their independence, Washington, the beloved Commander in Chief of the Continental Army, had been unanimously chosen by the people as the first President of the newly created nation, the United States of America.

★ ★ ★ ★ ★ ★ ★ ★ ★ ★ ★ ★ ★ ★ ★ ★ ★ ★

The regular postage rate at the time these two stamps were issued was 5 cents a half ounce under 300 miles and 10 cents a half ounce if over 300 miles. At times, there being a shortage of 5 cent stamps, a 10 cent stamp was cut in half and each half used in place of a 5 cent stamp.

In 1875 the Post Office Department reprinted the stamps for display at the Centennial Exposition of 1876. This printing was made from new plates on white paper, and the ungummed stamps were not good for postal use. The original printing had been on a paper of bluish tint.

The stamps of the Issue of 1847 were all imperforate.

On different copies of the same stamps, variations often occur. These varieties are of interest to a stamp collector. The variations, which may be either very slight or major ones, can be found on stamps of many of the issues. A variety may be due to different methods of printing or to the use of different kinds of paper or different shades of color. The plate from which the stamps are printed may become worn or scratched, or be recut. A shift in the transfer roll when making the plate will cause varieties.

Stamps are printed in sheets with a narrow space left between each stamp on the sheet. In order to be separated they then had to be cut apart and this involved a great deal of labor. Stamps that must be so cut apart are said to be imperforated, or "imperf." It was not until the second government issue that small holes, or perforations, in a straight line were placed between the stamps on the sheet so that they could easily be torn apart. These are perforate, or "perf.," stamps.

In classifying stamps the fact of no perforation or the number of perforations in two centimeters is a guide in determining the exact variety. Information as to the varieties can be found in a stamp catalogue.

Issue of 1851–60

BENJAMIN FRANKLIN

As the postal system grew, stamps of different values were needed and a second series was issued varying from 1 cent to 90 cents. The first Postmaster General and the first President are again pictured. On the 5 cent stamp of this issue Thomas Jefferson appears. Jefferson was one of the group of great statesmen, men of faith and courage, who built up the framework of our government dedicated to the proposition that all men are created equal. Jefferson had helped draft the Declaration of Independence and served as the third President of the United States.

Besides the regular stamps, two Carriers Stamps were issued. These are both of 1 cent value and were to be used in addition to the regular postage if a letter was to be delivered.

This series was first issued imperf. with the exception of the 24, 30, and 90 cent stamps, which were not regularly issued imperf. In 1857 perforations were used for the first time. This was the only time stamps were issued perf. 15, because it was found that stamps with fifteen perforations tore apart too easily.

Advanced stamp collectors find much interest in studying the many varieties which occur on the 1, 3, and 10 cent stamps of this series.

GEORGE WASHINGTON

THOMAS JEFFERSON

GEORGE WASHINGTON

GEORGE WASHINGTON

GEORGE WASHINGTON

BENJAMIN FRANKLIN

GEORGE WASHINGTON

CARRIERS' STAMPS

Early Cancellations

Early American stamps are found canceled in different ways. A postmaster had to provide his own canceling device. Sitting on a stool at his high desk, he scratched a few downstrokes with his quill pen or wrote his initials across the face of the stamp in order to cancel it; or he used a crude hand stamp carved from a small block of wood, or even a bottle cork with a design cut in it. From 1850 to 1870 each postmaster used any design he pleased, so that covers of the period carry cancellations of strange shapes and forms. There are designs of stars, grids, shields, circles and flags, bees, eagles, and even a running chicken and a kicking donkey. Later a standardized cancellation was used in all post offices.

Besides the cancellation marks, often there are postmarks indicating how the letter traveled to its destination. The word "Way" is found written or stamped on some early covers. This indicated that the letter had not been mailed at a post office but had been picked up by a carrier along the way and, with the payment of an extra fee, taken to the nearest post office.

THE MIDDLE DUTCH CHURCH USED ABOUT 1845 AS NEW YORK CITY POST OFFICE

Overland Mail and Pony Express

When the steamboat and the locomotive replaced the stagecoach, the mail between the Eastern cities and towns traveled over inland waterways and railroads. But there was no regular mail route over the thousands of miles of unsettled country between the East and the West.

In 1849 came the news of gold discovered in California. On foot, on pack horse, in covered wagon, gold-mad people pushed westward. Soon came the demand for a fast mail route from coast to coast. In 1858 the railroad west from St. Louis had reached Tipton, Missouri. The Government mail route up to this time, from the east to California, was by water to Panama, then by mule pack across the Isthmus and up the coast by boat. In order to speed the transportation of mail, John Butterfield, the founder of the American Express Company, organized the Butterfield Overland Mail and received a Government contract to transport United States mail overland by stagecoach from Tipton, Missouri, to San Francisco. The route was through the south by way of El Paso, Tucson, and Los Angeles to San Francisco. The schedule beginning in 1858 was twenty-five days.

With the coming of the Civil War, Congress transferred the service to the central route, through Salt Lake City, the western terminus becoming Placerville, California. In spite of attacks by Indians and highwaymen, the service was continued until the completion of the transcontinental railroad in 1869. The cost per letter for this overland mail service was 10 cents, but it had been figured that the cost to the Government was as much as eighty dollars a letter.

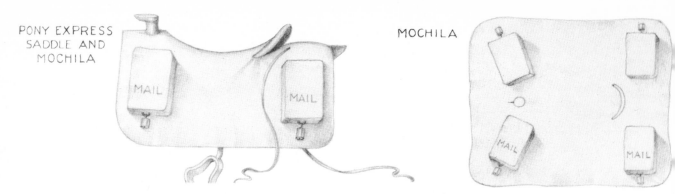

PONY EXPRESS
SADDLE AND
MOCHILA

MOCHILA

In order to carry mail still faster, the firm of Russell, Majors and Waddell operated the famed Pony Express between St. Joseph, Missouri, and Sacramento, California, beginning April 3, 1860.

Eighty fearless young riders, with mail in four locked pockets of the mochila, sped on, day and night, through wilderness and Indian territory. Each rider, on a fast, wiry pony, covered a distance of fifty to seventy-five miles, stopping only long enough to fling himself and the mail from his worn-out pony to the fresh one kept saddled and waiting for him every eight to twelve miles.

The rate charged by Russell, Majors and Waddell was $5.00 for a half ounce letter and the fee was evidenced by hand-stamped cancellations on the envelope. Toward the close, the rate was reduced to $1.00. Each letter also required a 10 cent Government stamp.

The Pony Express paved the way for the transcontinental telegraph which followed and inspired the building of the transcontinental railroad. When the telegraph was completed on October 24, 1861, the Pony Express came to an end. Its riders had ridden 650,000 miles, had lost only one mail, and only one of them had been killed by Indians.

Issues of 1861–66

The third series of stamps was issued at a sad time in United States history. The Southern slaveholding states had withdrawn from the Union and there was civil war. The Post Office Department in Washington recalled all unused postage stamps that had been issued up to this time, and they became worthless for postage. To replace them this new issue was brought out.

| BENJAMIN FRANKLIN | GEORGE WASHINGTON | THOMAS JEFFERSON | GEORGE WASHINGTON |
| GEORGE WASHINGTON | GEORGE WASHINGTON | BENJAMIN FRANKLIN | GEORGE WASHINGTON |

Because of changes in postal rates two additional denominations were added to this series, a 2 cent in 1863 and a 15 cent value in 1866.

On the 2 cent stamp, called the "Black Jack," is the stern, sad face of Andrew Jackson. General Jackson had saved New Orleans in the War of 1812. He had twice been President of the United States.

ANDREW JACKSON   ABRAHAM LINCOLN

The 15 cent denomination carries the portrait of Abraham Lincoln. This stamp was printed in black and was issued one year after the assassination of the great Civil War President. Although not issued as a memorial stamp, this 15 cent Lincoln is often classed as our first memorial stamp.

It was with this series that grills were first used. Different methods were tried out to avoid the possibility of stamps being reused for postage. One of these methods was a device called a grill. This consisted of a steel roller the surface of which was cut into a series of points. When the printed sheets of stamps were passed under the roller, the grill made indentations slightly breaking the paper surface of the stamp so that the canceling ink would soak in and could not be removed without destroying the stamp itself. It was found that, when the grill was placed all over the stamp, the paper was so weakened that often the stamp was torn while being separated along the perforations, and so grills of smaller area were experimented with. However, the use of the grill was abandoned by 1873.

The series of 1861 was issued without grills and from 1867 was also grilled in various sizes, including a 3 cent grilled all over.

In 1875 the series was reissued for the Centennial Exposition of 1876. The stamps were gummed and were good for postage.

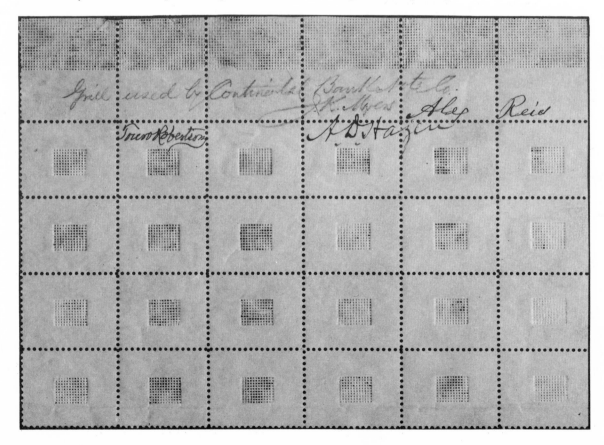

The Confederate Stamps of 1861–64

The Southern States which had withdrawn from the Union organized their own postal department and issued their own stamps. Until these Confederate stamps were available, the Southern postmasters used hand stamps, or Provisional stamps, just as the various postmasters had done before the first government issue.

Confederate stamps were brought out with greatest difficulty. In the war-torn South inadequate printing presses, poor inks and paper, caused many varieties. When proper printing ink could not be obtained, stamps were even printed from black ink made of carbon from the root of the grapevine.

Some issues of the Confederate stamps were printed in England and these reached the Southern States only if the ships carrying them could successfully run the blockade.

Examples of Postmasters' Provisionals

Several of the Confederate stamps carry the portrait of Jefferson Davis, who was the President of the Confederate States. Thomas Jefferson and George Washington and Andrew Jackson, men loved by both the North and the South, are also pictured on these stamps, as is the statesman from South Carolina, John Calhoun. The 1 cent stamp, which was printed in London and brought to the Confederate States by a blockade runner, was never placed in circulation.

JEFFERSON DAVIS   THOMAS JEFFERSON   ANDREW JACKSON   JEFFERSON DAVIS

ANDREW JACKSON   JEFFERSON DAVIS   JEFFERSON DAVIS   GEORGE WASHINGTON

JOHN C. CALHOUN

During the Civil War there were times when no envelopes could be had because of the scarcity of paper in the South. Among the collections of Civil War covers are envelopes of wrapping paper which had been stuck together with molasses instead of gum. Envelopes can be found that have been reused and have postal markings on the inside as well as on the outside, because the envelope had been turned, readdressed, and re-stamped. There are Civil War covers made from wallpaper torn from the walls by soldiers who could obtain paper in no other way.

Covers marked "Flag of Truce" and "Prisoner's Letter" crossed the lines between the North and the South. These often carried both United States and Confederate stamps. The cancellations on covers from the different prison camps are a record of a sad era in America's history.

After four and one-half years of war, peace came and the country was reunited; hence the need for Confederate stamps was over.

Issue of 1869

The stamps before this had carried portraits. This is the first series using pictures as well. The series was in use only a short time, for it was not popular—perhaps because of the smaller size of the stamps or because they were so different in design.

At the time the series was issued, the first railroad across the country had been completed. There was no longer any need for the post rider shown on the 2 cent stamp. Mail was now carried on trains pulled by locomotives pouring black smoke and sparks from great smokestacks, as pictured on the 3 cent stamp. In place of sailing ships steamships now carried mail across the seas, and the 12 cent stamp pictures the *S. S. Adriatic.* The 15 cent and 24 cent stamps picture two events from the story of America: the landing of Columbus, and a group of America's first statesmen signing the Declaration of Independence. A coat of arms is shown on the 10 cent and 30 cent stamps. The portraits of Franklin, Washington, and Lincoln appear on the 1 cent, 6 cent, and 90 cent values.

The 15, 24, 30, and 90 cent stamps of the series were printed in two colors, and so each sheet of stamps had to go through the press twice. Due to a printing error a few sheets of the 15 and 24 cent stamps were issued with the picture upside down. On a few sheets of the 30 cent stamp the flags were inverted. Inverted copies of these three stamps are very rare and valuable. There is no known invert of the 90 cent stamp.

In 1875 the series was reissued for the Centennial Exposition of 1876. The stamps were without grills, gummed, and were good for postage. In 1880 the 1 cent value was reissued again.

Bank Note Issues of 1870–87

The stamps of this series are larger in size and of a new classic design. They, like the early issues, carry pictures of Americans who played an important part in the building of the nation.

Several new faces appear for the first time. Edwin Stanton, honored on the 7 cent stamp, was Lincoln's Secretary of War during the Civil War. The Senator and orator Henry Clay is on the 12 cent stamp. The 15 cent value shows Daniel Webster, a brilliant orator and lawyer. A general of the War of 1812, Winfield Scott, nicknamed "Fuss and Feathers," is on the 24 cent stamp; and on the 30 cent value is Alexander Hamilton, who built the framework of our financial system and was the first Secretary of the Treasury.

BENJAMIN FRANKLIN

ANDREW JACKSON

GEORGE WASHINGTON

ABRAHAM LINCOLN

EDWIN M. STANTON

THOMAS JEFFERSON

HENRY CLAY

DANIEL WEBSTER

WINFIELD SCOTT

ALEXANDER HAMILTON

OLIVER HAZARD PERRY

The 90 cent stamp honors Commodore Perry. After victory over the British squadron in the war of 1812 he sent this message to the President, "We have met the enemy and they are ours: two ships, two brigs, one schooner, and one sloop."

ZACHARY TAYLOR

JAMES GARFIELD

Added to this series in 1875 was a new 5 cent denomination, to meet the new foreign postage rate. On it appears the portrait of Zachary Taylor. General Taylor, "Old Rough and Ready" as he was called, had fought many successful battles in the Indian Wars and had been our twelfth President. After the assassination of President Garfield in 1881, the Zachary Taylor 5 cent stamp was replaced by a Garfield 5 cent stamp, honoring the late President.

In 1883 the postage rate on first-class mail was reduced from 3 cents to 2 cents for each half ounce, and a newly designed 2 cent stamp with a bust of Washington was issued. A 4 cent denomination bearing the head of Jackson and a new 1 cent Franklin with a more nearly uniform frame were also issued.

In the 1870 series secret marks put in by the printer can be found. The National Bank Note Company first printed the series. In 1873, when the contract for printing went to the Continental Bank Note Company, later merged with and known as the American Bank Note Company, tiny secret marks were added in the border design to distinguish this company's work from that of its predecessor.

Grills were used here for the last time and the later issues of this series appear without grills.

GEORGE WASHINGTON

ANDREW JACKSON

BENJAMIN FRANKLIN

Issues of 1890-93

BENJAMIN FRANKLIN   GEORGE WASHINGTON   ANDREW JACKSON

ABRAHAM LINCOLN   ULYSSES S. GRANT   JAMES GARFIELD   WILLIAM T. SHERMAN

DANIEL WEBSTER   HENRY CLAY   THOMAS JEFFERSON   OLIVER HAZARD PERRY

     The stamps of this series are smaller than those of previous issues. Added to the portraits of the Americans honored before are two of the greatest Union generals of the Civil War. On the 5 cent stamp is pictured Ulysses Grant, who, after the end of the war, served as President for two terms. In 1893 a new registry rate called for a stamp of 8 cent value. This 8 cent stamp carries the portrait of William T. Sherman, who, having cut his way through the heart of the South and taken the city of Savannah, sent this message to President Lincoln: "I beg to present you as a Christmas gift the city of Savannah."

Columbian Issue of 1893

To commemorate the 400th anniversary of the discovery of America by Columbus.
In connection with the World's Columbian Exposition held in Chicago in 1893.

This is the first commemorative series of United States stamps. The pictures on the stamps are from paintings showing events in the life of Christopher Columbus.

In the time of Columbus many thought that the earth was flat, and the sea filled with monsters ready to gobble up the ships. Superstitious sailors feared they would fall into space if they sailed too far. But Cristoforo Colombo, the Italian navigator and map maker whom we know as Christopher Columbus, believed the earth to be round and was sure he could reach the rich lands of India by sailing westward. Having secured the aid of the Spanish court, Columbus set out on his voyage of discovery.

The 1 cent stamp pictures Columbus in sight of land. After a voyage of many weeks, with the sailors ready to mutiny and terrified because of the long distance they had come, one of the crew shouted from the rigging that land was in sight. However, Columbus himself claimed that previously he had seen a moving light and so had been the first to sight land.

On the 2 cent value is shown the landing of Columbus with his officers and men. The landing was made on an island of the Bahamas called by the natives "Guanahani." On the morning of October 12, 1492, Columbus, with the banner of Spain in his hand, claimed the newly discovered land for King Ferdinand and Queen Isabella.

The flagship of Columbus is pictured on the 3 cent stamp. This ship he christened the *Santa Maria* and it was the largest of his fleet.

The 4 cent stamp shows a picture of the little fleet of three sailing ships, the *Santa Maria* and the tiny *Pinta* and *Nina*. The *Santa Maria* was wrecked while Columbus was exploring further the unknown waters about the land he had discovered. Columbus then returned to Spain.

The picture on the 5 cent stamp shows Columbus soliciting Queen Isabella's aid for his proposed voyage over unknown seas. It was only after many disappointments in finding anyone to back him that he at last had the opportunity of laying his plans before the Spanish queen.

The stamp of 6 cent denomination pictures the proud entry of Columbus into the city of Barcelona on his triumphant return to Spain. The discoverer was welcomed by great throngs of cheering people gathered along the highway to the city.

Columbus fitted out a new fleet and made a second voyage to the New World. When the riches for which the Spanish court had hoped from the discovery did not materialize, there were times when Columbus was discredited. The 8 cent stamp shows him restored to royal favor after having been brought back to Spain in chains.

The 10 cent denomination pictures Columbus presenting the Spanish king and queen with gifts he brought from the newly found land. Copper-skinned natives (called Indians by Columbus), gay-colored parrots, mysterious cotton plants, and nuggets of gold were presented to the court.

The 15 cent stamp shows Columbus on the return from his voyage as he announces his discovery to Ferdinand and Isabella. In his report to his royal sponsors he told of the vast treasures to be found in the New World he had discovered.

On the stamp of 30 cent denomination the navigator Columbus is shown at the Spanish Convent of Rabida before he had succeeded in finding anyone to back his plan for the first voyage. At Rabida he made friends with the friar Jean Perez, who did much to help Columbus gain Isabella's aid.

At first Columbus had not been able to interest King Ferdinand and Queen Isabella in his plan of finding a direct route to India. Discouraged, he had left the Spanish court to try elsewhere. The 50 cent stamp pictures his recall to the court by a messenger who announced to him that Queen Isabella had reversed her decision.

The stamp of $1 denomination shows the Queen as she pledges her jewels to obtain money for the voyage proposed by Columbus. Spain had long been at war with the Moors, and the Spanish treasury had little money.

Columbus made a second voyage to the land which he believed to be India and was appointed "Viceroy of the Indies." King Ferdinand then sent one of his officers to investigate the new lands. Listening to rumors, this officer of the King had Columbus thrown into prison and sent back to Spain. The $2 stamp pictures Columbus in chains.

On the stamp of $3 denomination the discoverer is pictured as he tells the court of the third voyage he made to the New World. During this voyage he had sailed along the northern shore of South America and had seen the American mainland for the first time.

Portraits of the Spanish queen and Columbus appear on the stamp of $4 denomination. It was her help that made the voyages of Columbus possible.

The $5 stamp pictures the gray-haired Columbus. After his last attempt to make a settlement in the New World and secure the riches and wealth for which the Spanish court was waiting, the discoverer returned to Spain ill and discouraged. He died in semipoverty thinking he had reached India, not knowing that he had discovered two great new continents.

"Bureau Issues" of 1894–99

Beginning with this issue, the printing of stamps was taken out of the hands of private contractors and transferred to the Bureau of Engraving and Printing in Washington, hence the name "Bureau Issues."

This series closely resembles the series of 1890, but can be identified by triangles added to the upper corners of the design.

BENJAMIN FRANKLIN GEORGE WASHINGTON ANDREW JACKSON ABRAHAM LINCOLN

ULYSSES S. GRANT JAMES GARFIELD WILLIAM T. SHERMAN DANIEL WEBSTER

HENRY CLAY THOMAS JEFFERSON OLIVER HAZARD PERRY JAMES MADISON

JOHN MARSHALL

James Madison and John Marshall are added to the men who have already appeared on other issues. Madison, the fourth President of the United States, is on the $2 stamp. The $5 stamp honors John Marshall, one of the greatest American jurists and a Chief Justice of the Supreme Court.

The Bureau stamps were first issued unwatermarked. In 1895 water-marks were introduced. To make the counterfeiting of stamps more difficult, a watermarked paper was manufactured on which to print the stamps.

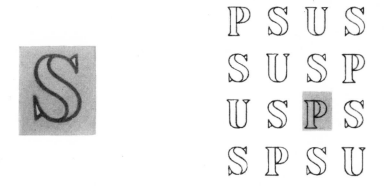

The double-line letters U.S.P.S. (United States Postal Service) were arranged so that each stamp showed one complete letter or parts of a letter. This watermark appears on all United States stamps from 1895 to 1910.

In 1910 a single-line watermark, U.S.P.S., was introduced. The letters here were arranged so that a small portion of several letters is often all that can be seen on any one stamp. Watermarks were discontinued in 1916.

In 1898 the United States Post Office Department agreed to adopt prescribed colors for certain postal rates as decided upon by the Universal Postal Union. The colors were similar to those of corresponding rates of different countries. This caused a change in the color of the 1 cent and 5 cent stamp. Later the colors of the 4, 6, 10, and 15 cent stamps were also changed, to avoid the possible confusion resulting from different denominations being printed in nearly the same colors. Since that time the ordinary 1 cent stamp has been green; a stamp of 5 cent value, blue.

Trans-Mississippi Issue of 1898

To commemorate the settling of the Middle West. In connection with the Trans-Mississippi Exposition held in Omaha, Nebraska, in 1898.

The stamps of this series show the development of the vast Middle West. The early settlements in America had been along the Eastern coast, but the daring and sturdy pioneers continually moved on westward.

In 1673, when even in the East there were but few scattered settlements, Père Marquette ventured into the wild, unknown Western territory. Marquette, a French Jesuit priest and a friend of the Indians, was among the first to explore the treacherous winding Mississippi River.

The broad expanse of level land of the Middle West became the wheatland of our country. On the 2 cent stamp is an engraving of farm machinery drawn by horses, as it was at the time these stamps were issued.

The shaggy bison, or buffalo, pictured on the 4 cent value roamed the great Western prairies in herds. This mighty animal had supplied food for the Indians, who used its hide for their clothing and tepees. As the West developed, the settlers shot so many of the buffalo that they were fast disappearing.

The great Western barrier of the Rocky Mountains was explored by John Charles Frémont in 1842. The 5 cent stamp shows Captain Frémont as he placed the American flag on one of the highest peaks. He mapped much of the Western territory and opened trails for the great stream of settlers moving westward.

The early pioneers who followed the trails suffered untold hardships. United States soldiers appear on the 8 cent stamp guarding a long line of covered wagons in danger from attacking Indians.

The 10 cent stamp pictures a lone covered wagon which has met with tragic misfortune.

On the 50 cent value the picture of a prospector, with his burros, searching for gold, and on the $1 stamp the beautiful engraving of cattle lost in a blinding snowstorm—both portray part of the Western story.

The $2 stamp shows a great railroad bridge spanning the Mississippi River at the city of St. Louis, the gateway to the West.

Pan-American Issue of 1901

To commemorate the Pan-American Exposition held at Buffalo, New York, in 1901.

On each of the stamps of this series is an engraving of a great engineering achievement of the time. Fast steamers plied the Great Lakes. On the New York Central Railroad the Empire State Express roared along at sixty miles an hour. On the highways was to be seen a strange-looking horseless carriage which ran by electricity. The largest single-span bridge in the world had been built at Niagara Falls. At Sault Sainte Marie, Michigan, engineers had constructed great ship-canal locks, through which ships laden with wheat passed from one of the Great Lakes to another. Across the ocean, steamships were bringing a stream of emigrants who were to become Americans.

Some of the greatest rarities among United States stamps are found in the Pan-American issue. The series was printed in two colors and, due to an error in printing, a few sheets of the 1 cent and 2 cent stamps had the picture upside down in the frame. A few inverts of the 4 cent stamp have also come into the hands of collectors.

Issues of 1902–17

This issue is beautiful in color and elaborate in design. Many shades of color and many varieties occur. Some of the Americans appearing on earlier issues are again pictured here, with the addition of Martha Washington on the 8 cent denomination and Benjamin Harrison on the 13 cent. Harrison had been a general in the Civil War and President of the United States for one term. On the $1 stamp the great sea fighter Admiral Farragut is pictured.

The 2 cent stamp was criticized because of the crowded frame and the prominent nose in Washington's portrait, so it was discontinued and a new 2 cent Washington design took its place in 1903.

The $2 and $5 stamps were first issued watermarked perf. 12 and reissued in 1917 unwatermarked perf. 10.

BENJAMIN FRANKLIN

GEORGE WASHINGTON

ANDREW JACKSON

ULYSSES S. GRANT

ABRAHAM LINCOLN

JAMES GARFIELD

MARTHA WASHINGTON

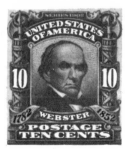

DANIEL WEBSTER

BENJAMIN HARRISON

HENRY CLAY

THOMAS JEFFERSON

DAVID G. FARRAGUT

JAMES MADISON

JOHN MARSHALL

GEORGE WASHINGTON

With this series, imperforate stamps were regularly issued for the first time since the 1851 issue. The 1, 5, and 2 cents stamps were brought out imperf. From the sheets of imperf. stamps the Post Office Department manufactured coil stamps by perforating the sheets, either horizontally or vertically, and then cutting them into strips of 20 stamps and pasting the strips together to form rolls of 500 stamps. Coil stamps are for use in stamp-vending machines.

Louisiana Purchase Issue of 1904

To commemorate the 100th anniversary of the purchase of Louisiana Territory. In connection with the World's Fair held in St. Louis, Missouri, in 1904.

One hundred years before this series was issued, a huge unexplored territory, stretching from the Mississippi River to the far West, was owned by France. At that time Western farmers of the United States floated their produce down the river to the French city of New Orleans and were often in serious trouble with the French and Spanish settlers. President Thomas Jefferson, fearing that the French would close off the use of the river, negotiated with France to buy the island of New Orleans. To everyone's surprise Napoleon offered to sell the whole great territory of Louisiana for the sum of fifteen million dollars. The sale was carried through and, by this purchase, the United States was doubled in size.

Men connected with the negotiations are honored on this issue of stamps—as is President William McKinley, who was assassinated in 1901.

On the 1 cent denomination is the portrait of Robert Livingston, United States Minister to France, who was in charge of the negotiations. Thomas Jefferson, President at the time of purchase, is on the 2 cent stamp. The 3 cent denomination carries the portrait of James Monroe, Special Ambassador to France, who assisted in the negotiations of purchase. William McKinley is on the 5 cent stamp, and on the 10 cent value is a map showing the vast area of land included in the purchase.

A POST OFFICE IN LOUISIANA TERRITORY

Jamestown Issue of 1907

To commemorate the 300th anniversary of the founding of Jamestown. In connection with the Exposition held at Hampton Roads, Virginia, in 1907.

In the year 1607 a group of one hundred and twenty English "adventurers" set sail for the New World. They reached the Virginia coast and sailed up a broad river which they named the James, in honor of the King. On its banks they chose a site for the settlement, and called it Jamestown.

Many of these colonists knew nothing of pioneering or how to live in a wilderness. They had insufficient supplies and the Indians were hostile. Half of the little colony died from starvation and disease before supplies and more colonists arrived from England. Through the "starving time" and through the "Great Massacre" by the Indians, Jamestown survived and was the first permanent English settlement in America.

The leader of the group was the sturdy, resourceful Captain John Smith, whose portrait is on the 1 cent stamp. He forced all the colonists to work. He explored the surrounding country. The story tells that, when he was captured by the Indians, his life was saved by Pocahontas, the great Chief Powhatan's young daughter, who threw herself between him and an Indian's upraised hatchet.

Pocahontas married John Rolfe, one of the Jamestown colonists, and went with him to England, where she was presented to the King and Queen. Pocahontas, or Rebecca Rolfe as she was renamed, died in England when only twenty-two years old. The 5 cent stamp is from a portrait of Pocahontas dressed in Elizabethan clothes.

Washington—Franklin Issues of 1908–19

This new regular series of stamps, issued in a beautiful range of colors, was in use for many years. Only Washington and Franklin appear on the stamps, which are simple and nearly identical in design. The stamps were issued in many major varieties. Different types of paper were used and changes occur in watermarks, color, and perforations. The single-line watermark was introduced in this series.

The many different printings, of flat plate, offset, rotary press, and coils, make classification of the stamps of this series interesting for the stamp collector.

In 1908 twelve stamps were issued, with Franklin's portrait appearing on the 1 cent value and Washington's on all the other values—the 2, 3, 4, 5, 6, 8, 10, 13, 15, and 50 cent stamps and the $1 stamp.

In 1912 a new set of this issue was brought out. This time both the 1 and 2 cent denominations portrayed Washington, and the values were expressed in numerals instead of in written words. On the denominations from 8 cents to $1 the portrait of Franklin was used.

From time to time new denominations were added to the series as conditions warranted.

In 1918 new $2 and $5 stamps were issued. These were horizontal in shape, instead of vertical, and printed in two colors. A portrait of Franklin was also used on these denominations.

The famous 5 cent red error occurs in this issue. Due to a platemaker's mistake some sheets of 2 cent stamps, printed from a repaired plate, contained three stamps of 5 cent denomination. These 5 cent stamps appeared, of course, in the same red color as the 2 cent stamps on the sheet. The error was discovered by a puzzled Virginia postmaster, who wrote to the Post Office Department asking what he should charge for the stamp marked 5 cents but found in a sheet of 2 cent stamps. Immediately the misprinted sheets were recalled, but some of the "5 cent errors" were already in the hands of the public.

Lincoln Memorial Issue of 1909

A memorial stamp in commemoration of the 100th anniversary of the birth of Abraham Lincoln, February 12, 1809.

Abe Lincoln, one of the greatest of all Americans, was a boy of the frontier, born in a log cabin in Kentucky. Honest Abe, the young self-taught lawyer, became President Lincoln just before the Civil War. He worked unceasingly to hold the Union of the States together. He issued the proclamation freeing the slaves and guided the nation through the troubled years of the war.

A few days after the surrender of the Confederate Army, while Washington was celebrating the end of the war, President Lincoln was assassinated.

Americans humbly and proudly honor the simple, great man who declared at Gettysburg "that we here highly resolve that these dead shall not have died in vain—that this nation, under God, shall have a new birth of freedom—and that government of the people, by the people, for the people shall not perish from the earth."

The portrait on the stamp is from a statue of Lincoln, by Saint-Gaudens, which now stands in Grant Park, Chicago.

Issued perf. and imperf. on regular white paper and perf. on a paper of bluish tinge.

BIRTH-PLACE
OF LINCOLN

Alaska–Yukon Issue of 1909

To commemorate the development of the Alaska–Yukon–Pacific Territory which was celebrated by an exposition at Seattle, Washington, in 1909.

The vast land of Alaska became a part of the United States of America through the efforts of William Seward, the man pictured on this stamp. He was Lincoln's farseeing Secretary of State. In 1867 Seward negotiated the purchase of Alaska from Russia for $7,200,000. At the time, Alaska was referred to as "Seward's icebox" and few realized either the wealth of its natural resources or its great possibilities.

The design first submitted for this stamp portrayed a seal on a cake of ice. It was quickly rejected, lest it give the impression that Alaska is a land of only ice and snow.

This stamp was issued perf. and imperf., double-line watermark.

Hudson–Fulton Issue of 1909

*To commemorate the 300th anniversary of Henry Hudson's discovery of
the Hudson River and the 100th anniversary of its first navigation by steam.*

This stamp pictures an Indian canoe, which was the first craft on the river, together with Henry Hudson's *Half Moon* and Robert Fulton's steamboat, the *Clermont*.

In 1609 Henry Hudson, an English navigator in the employ of the Dutch, was searching along the Eastern coast of the New World for a passageway through to India. He found the mouth of a large river and sailed up its course until it became too shallow for navigation. The next year, still in search of the Northwest Passage, he explored the icy waters of Hudson's Bay. Here he and his young son were set adrift by his mutinous crew and were never heard of again. The river and the bay still carry Hudson's name.

Two hundred years after the *Half Moon* sailed the Hudson, many settlements and towns had grown up along its banks. One day in 1809 jeering crowds of people gathered to see the trial trip of a strange-looking craft which its builder, Robert Fulton, claimed could be navigated by steam. They watched as clouds of smoke and fiery sparks poured from the thirty-foot smokestack. Against the wind and the tide Fulton's steamboat moved steadily up the river. In thirty-two hours "Fulton's Folly," as the *Clermont* was called, made the trip to Albany—and steamboat navigation was established in America.

Issued both perf. and imperf., double-line watermark.

Panama–Pacific Issue of 1912–15

To commemorate the opening of the Panama Canal and the discovery of the Pacific Ocean. In connection with the Panama Pacific Exposition, San Francisco, 1915.

The 1 cent stamp honors the Spanish explorer Balboa, who was the first white man to see the Pacific Ocean from the east. Balboa had heard the Indians tell of a "Great Water" and of pearls and gold on the other side of the Panama Isthmus. With a group of Spaniards and a few Indians, Balboa set out in 1513 to find this "Great Water"— hoping, with a new discovery, to win back the favor of the Spanish king. The party hacked their way through the vine-tangled jungle, where lurked poisonous reptiles and wild animals. In the terrific heat they succeeded in crossing the isthmus and at last came out in sight of the Pacific Ocean.

Four hundred years later, through these same mountains and jungles, the Panama Canal was built, connecting the world's largest oceans. This great piece of engineering was accomplished by an American army engineer, Colonel Goethals. The 2 cent stamp shows a warship and a merchant ship in one of the canal locks.

The 5 cent stamp pictures a glowing Western sunset over the rocks of the Golden Gate. Between these rocks lies the opening from the San Francisco harbor into the Pacific Ocean.

It is believed that in 1769 a Spanish governor of Lower California stumbled upon the great landlocked water called San Francisco Bay. Accompanied by several priests and a group of Spanish and Indian hunters, he was exploring the California coastline. The 10 cent stamp shows the scene of this discovery.

The series was perf. 10 in 1915.

Victory Issue of 1919

To commemorate the successful outcome of World War I.

The design on the stamp symbolizes a victorious Liberty with the scales of justice in one hand and a naked sword in the other.

The United States flag is placed at the top and behind the figure. The flags of the two powers next in greatness, Great Britain and France, are in front and on either side. The Belgian and Italian flags are in the background, the Belgian flag first as Belgium was the first to fight in the war.

When the four years of the first World War came to a close in 1918 it was fervently believed that the allied victory would bring peace to the ravaged world.

Pilgrim Tercentenary Issue of 1920

In commemoration of the 300th anniversary of the landing of the Pilgrims in 1620.

It was the *Mayflower*, the little sailing vessel honored on the 1 cent stamp, that brought the Pilgrims to America. The Pilgrims had fled to Holland because they differed with the Church of England. Not content there, they came to the New World. The *Mayflower* sailed from Plymouth, England, early in September, 1620, with about one hundred colonists crowded on the little vessel.

Winter had set in when the *Mayflower* anchored in the Bay of Cape Cod and the band of Pilgrims chose a spot for settlement which they called Plymouth. On the edge of the wilderness they built bark-covered shacks to shelter them from the cold of that first New England winter, from the Indians, and from the wolves of the forest. The Pilgrims were the first settlers in Massachusetts. The landing is pictured on the 2 cent value.

Just before leaving the *Mayflower*, the men gathered together in its tiny cabin and drew up and signed a solemn pact. They agreed to make just and equal laws and promised to obey the laws. This agreement is the Mayflower Compact, the signing of which is pictured on the 5 cent stamp.

Issues of 1922–25

As the similarity in the Washington–Franklin series of ordinary stamps had proved confusing to the postal clerks handling the mail, a new regular series was issued with more variations in design, size, and color.

Americans not before pictured on our stamps are included here. On the ½ cent denomination is Nathan Hale, the patriot who gave his life as a spy with the words "I only regret that I have but one life to lose for my country." Warren Harding, who served as President, appears on the 1½ cent stamp.

On the 5 cent denomination is the portrait of the strong-minded, positive Theodore Roosevelt, who organized the regiment of "Rough Riders" in the Spanish–American War and who served as President of the United States for two terms. Rutherford Hayes, pictured on the 11 cent stamp, had been a general in the Civil War before he was President. The 12 cent stamp pictures Grover Cleveland, twice President of the United States. The picture of the American Indian on the 14 cent stamp is from a likeness of a Sioux Indian named Hollow Horn Bear.

The stamps of the higher denominations of the series carry pictures instead of portraits. The Statue of Liberty, the buffalo, and the scenes and buildings pictured are all part of America.

The series was printed flat plate and rotary press. Some of the stamps were issued imperf. and in coil form.

Harding Memorial Issue of 1923

A special 2 cent stamp printed in black ink was issued in memory of Warren Harding, who had served in the Senate and as President of the United States. President Harding died while in office.

This stamp was issued flat plate perf. and imperf., and rotary press perf. only.

Issues of 1925–26

A new 17 cent denomination was issued bearing a portrait of Woodrow Wilson, President during the first World War. Woodrow Wilson envisioned a new world order and expressed his ideals in the "Fourteen Points," thus laying the foundation for a League of Nations uniting all the world.

In 1926 Benjamin Harrison's portrait again appears—on a 13 cent denomination with design similar to that of the current series.

COLUMN ERECTED AT
MAYPORT BY RIBAULT

FROM DRAWING MADE IN 1564

Huguenot–Walloon Issue of 1924

*To commemorate the anniversaries of the settling of
the Huguenots and Walloons in the New World.*

In 1624 the Dutch ship *New Netherland*, shown
on the 1 cent stamp, brought a colony of Walloons
to America. The Walloons were Belgians of Prot-
estant faith who were in search of a place where
they could live and worship in peace.

The *New Netherland* sailed up the Hudson
River and a site was chosen for the colony, which
was called Fort Orange. This was where Albany,
New York, stands today. The Walloons were indus-
trious and sturdy colonists. They made friends with
the Indians, and Fort Orange prospered and was, at
the time, as important as New Amsterdam. The 2
cent stamp pictures the landing of the Walloons.

The 5 cent stamp pictures a monument at Mayport, Florida, in memory of a colony which had a
sadly different fate. Jean Ribaut and a group of
French Huguenots established a colony at Mayport
in 1562. The Spanish Governor of Florida, sworn to
drive all Protestants from the New World, massacred
this entire Huguenot colony.

Lexington — Concord Issue of 1925

To commemorate the 150th anniversary of the first battle of the Revolutionary War.

On the 1 cent stamp George Washington is shown standing under the Elm tree at Cambridge, Massachusetts, as he takes over the supreme command of the Continental Army. This was on July 3, 1775.

During a night in April, 1775, villagers and farmers in the countryside around Lexington and Concord were awakened with the news that the British were on their way from Boston to capture colonial arms and supplies. A small group of American patriots, armed with rifles, opposed the British on the Lexington Common but were overwhelmed, and the Redcoats marched on to the North Bridge at Concord. More Minutemen—patriots of Massachusetts banded together to fight at a moment's notice—had gathered here and the British were driven back in retreat to Boston. The first battle of the Revolutionary War had taken place. A painting of this is shown on the 2 cent stamp.

The picture shown on the 5 cent stamp is from a statue of "The Minute Man" in Concord. The inscription on the stamp is from a hymn written by Ralph Waldo Emerson:

> By the rude bridge that arched the flood,
> Their flag to April's breeze unfurled,
> Here once the embattled farmers stood,
> And fired the shot heard round the world.

Norse–American Issue of 1925

To commemorate the 100th anniversary of the arrival of the first Norwegian immigrants to America in 1825.

Fifty-two Norwegian Quakers pooled their money and bought the tiny sloop, *The Restaurationen*, shown on the 2 cent stamp, which brought them safely to America in 1825. With the aid of American Quakers they established in New York State the first Norwegian colony.

The Viking ship pictured on the 5 cent stamp is a copy of one discovered in an ancient burial mound in Norway. A daring Norwegian and his crew sailed this Viking ship from Norway to America at the time of the World's Columbian Exposition.

It was in such a tiny open boat with sail and oars that the Norseman Leif Ericson had reached America long before its discovery by Columbus.

The Norse–American stamps were printed in two colors.

Sesquicentennial Independence Issue of 1926

To commemorate the 150th anniversary of American Independence. In connection with the Sesquicentennial Exposition held in Philadelphia in 1926.

In 1751 the Philadelphia Fathers ordered a great bell to be cast in London and shipped to them, to hang in the new Philadelphia State House. Around the bell in large letters were to be the words from the Bible "Proclaim Liberty throughout all the land unto all the inhabitants thereof." The bell arrived, but when it was tried out a great crack appeared. It had to be recast twice before it was hung in the steeple of the State House.

The day came on July 8, 1776, when the bell did "Proclaim Liberty." The Declaration of Independence had just been read to the people in the Square of the Philadelphia State House when the great bell was rung, declaring that the Colonies of America were to be free and independent.

Years later the bell again cracked, when it was tolling the death of Chief Justice Marshall. It was removed from the steeple and now stands in Independence Hall, Philadelphia—a symbol of American Liberty.

The Liberty Bell is pictured on the stamp.

INDEPENDENCE HALL
THE STATE HOUSE   1776

Ericsson Memorial Issue of 1926

A memorial to John Ericsson. In connection with the unveiling of his statue by the Crown Prince of Sweden, at Washington, D. C.

John Ericsson was a Swedish-born marine inventor. During the Civil War he designed the *Monitor* for the U. S. Navy. It was a tiny, strange-looking battleship with deck close to the water and a turret with two revolving guns. This "Yankee cheesebox on a raft" was covered with sheets of iron. In a naval battle of the Civil War the *Monitor* clashed with the *Merrimac*, a Confederate vessel with iron plates built rooflike over its sides. This battle of ironclad boats changed naval warfare for all time.

As a tribute to John Ericsson the stamp was of 5 cent denomination, the letter rate to Sweden and other foreign countries.

White Plains Issue of 1926

To commemorate the 150th anniversary of the Battle of White Plains.

This stamp honors an American defeat in the War for Independence. The courageous stand at White Plains, New York, in 1777 allowed General Washington to withdraw his men to strategic ground. Young Alexander Hamilton was a Captain of Artillery in this battle, and one of his gun crews is pictured on the stamp—as is the Continental flag with its thirteen stars and the "Liberty or Death" flag, which was first used in this battle.

Besides the regular issue there was a special issue of miniature sheets, each sheet having twenty-five stamps. The souvenir sheets were printed and sold at the International Philatelic Exhibition in New York, 1926.

Vermont Sesquicentennial Issue of 1927

To commemorate the 150th anniversary of the Independence of Vermont and the Battle of Bennington.

The settlers of the "New Hampshire Grants," as Vermont was known in its early history, had a rugged fight to exist. Vermont was claimed by both New York and New Hampshire but refused to acknowledge the authority of either and, in 1777, declared its own independence.

The Battle of Bennington, Vermont, one of the important battles of the American Revolution, led to General Burgoyne's surrender. The stamp pictures one of the "Green Mountain Boys," as Vermont's fighting men were called.

Burgoyne Campaign Issue of 1927

To commemorate the Battles of Fort Stanwix, Oriskany, Bennington, and Saratoga.

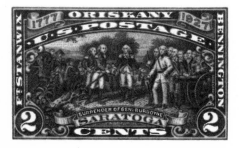

The successful outcome of the four battles of the Revolution commemorated on this stamp led to a great victory for the Americans. At Saratoga, the British General John Burgoyne was forced to surrender to the American Commander. If the campaign planned by General Burgoyne had succeeded, it would have cut off New England from the Southern States and would have meant disaster to the American cause. This stamp shows the scene of the surrender at Saratoga, in 1777.

Valley Forge Issue of 1928

To commemorate the 150th anniversary of the encampment of Washington's Army at Valley Forge.

In the winter of 1777–78, with the British forces occupying Philadelphia, Washington withdrew his tattered troops to Valley Forge and there encamped for the winter. The men were half starved, half frozen, and without shoes.

A friendly Quaker named Isaac Potts, at whose Valley Forge home Washington and his staff were stationed, came upon the general kneeling in the snow as he prayed for guidance in the darkest days of the War for Independence. The picture on the stamp is from a painting of this scene. The words "In God We Trust" are on this stamp. These words are on all our coins, but this is the only stamp on which they appear.

Hawaiian Overprinted Issue of 1928

To commemorate the 150th anniversary of the discovery of Hawaii by Captain Cook. Issued for sale in Hawaiian post offices; also sold at the Philatelic Agency in Washington.

This was a special issue of the current 2 and 5 cent stamps with the word "Hawaii" and the dates "1778–1928" overprinted in black. Few persons realized that these stamps could be used at any United States post office, because they were sold only in Hawaii and at the Philatelic Agency in Washington.

The islands of Hawaii were discovered by the English explorer Captain Cook. Captain Cook, in his ship with many white sails, was at first received by the natives of the islands as their white god, who had returned to them in a winged ship. On his second visit trouble arose between the natives and some of his crew, and Captain Cook was killed. During the following years several countries tried to get control of the islands. At their request the Hawaiian Islands were annexed to this country and became a part of the United States of America.

The Molly Pitcher Issue of 1928

To commemorate the 150th anniversary of the Battle of Monmouth.

This issue was an overprinted stamp with the name "Molly Pitcher" printed in black over an ordinary current 2 cent stamp.

Molly Pitcher, honored on this stamp, was a dauntless girl of Revolutionary times who followed her husband to the battlefield of Monmouth, where in the heat and dust of battle she carried fresh water back and forth to the thirsty and wounded soldiers. When her husband, a gunner, was killed during the battle, Molly Pitcher took his place and continued to fire the gun.

Aeronautics Conference Issue of 1928

To commemorate the 25th anniversary of the first flight of the Wright brothers, December 17, 1903. In connection with the International Civil Aeronautics Conference held in Washington, D. C., in 1928.

The 2 cent stamp shows the flying machine invented by Wilbur and Orville Wright. This was the first motor-powered, heavier-than-air plane to fly. It made its first successful flight at Kitty Hawk, N. C., in the face of the bitter wind of a cold December day in 1903. The machine, with Wilbur at the controls, moved down a runway constructed on the sandy beach and lifted itself into the air. Although the flight lasted but one minute, it proved to the world that man could fly.

A monoplane is pictured on the 5 cent stamp, and in the design of both stamps are the Washington monument and the United States Capitol.

George Rogers Clark Issue of 1929

To commemorate the 150th anniversary of the surrender of Fort Sackville, at Vincennes, Indiana, in 1779.

This stamp honors the young Virginia soldier who, more than any other, helped to win the Northwest Territory to the American cause. George Rogers Clark, with a group of volunteers, pushed his way westward through wilderness and forest. He fought hostile Indians and won over the French posts which had been established. Suddenly appearing at Fort Sackville, he misled the British commander as to the size of his force. The surrender of the British to Captain Clark, in 1779, is pictured on the stamp. This stamp was printed in two colors.

Edison Issue of 1929

To commemorate the 50th anniversary of the invention by Thomas Edison of the first incandescent electric lamp.

The first successful electric light was due to the tireless effort and experiments of Thomas Alva Edison. In an experiment in 1879 Edison watched a bit of cotton thread, which he had carbonized and sealed in a vacuum bulb, burn brightly for forty-five hours—and knew that lighting by electricity had become a fact.

As it is the custom of the Post Office Department not to picture a living person on United States stamps, the portrait of the great inventor did not appear but his first lamp is shown.

The Edison stamp was printed flat plate and rotary press, in sheet and coil form. This is the only commemorative stamp printed in coil form.

Sullivan Expedition Issue of 1929

To commemorate the 150th anniversary of the Sullivan Expedition.

In 1779 John Sullivan, a general in the Continental Army under George Washington, led a campaign against the savage Indians of the Six Nations, called the Iroquois, who were scalping and killing the settlers in New York State. Sullivan's expedition broke the power of the Iroquois and made the territory safe for the white settlements. The stamp pictures Major General John Sullivan.

State Overprinted Issue of 1929

An issue of stamps of the current 1922 series, in denominations of 1 cent to 10 cents, was overprinted with the abbreviations "Kans." or "Nebr." It was hoped that the overprint would prevent post-office burglars from selling stolen stamps in another state. The issue was tried out in Kansas and Nebraska. It was planned to extend the measure to other states, but after this one issue the idea was abandoned. In mail-order houses in other states, which often received stamps in payment, the overprinted stamps created considerable confusion.

Battle of Fallen Timbers Issue of 1929

A memorial to General Anthony Wayne and to commemorate the 135th anniversary of the Battle of Fallen Timbers.

Anthony Wayne with a frontiersman and an Indian are pictured on the stamp. The figures shown are from a monument erected to General Wayne at Fallen Timbers Park, Ohio.

After the Revolutionary War the lives of the white settlers in the Northwest Territory were in grave danger from the Indians. President Washington sent General Wayne to subdue the Indian country.

The campaign ended at Fallen Timbers among great forest trees uprooted by a hurricane. Here there was a large Indian encampment upon which General Wayne made an attack. After being routed, the Indians ceded more land to the white men and made a treaty with General Wayne.

Ohio Canalization Issue of 1929

To commemorate the completion of the Ohio River Canal System.

A system of locks and dams placed along the Ohio River between Cairo, Illinois, and Pittsburgh, Pennsylvania, turned the river into a great waterway navigable at all times of the year. The stamp shows a typical lock on the river.

Massachusetts Bay Colony Issue of 1930

To commemorate the 300th anniversary of
the founding of Massachusetts Bay Colony.

About ten years after the Pilgrims landed at Plymouth, another group of English colonists settled in New England under the sponsorship of the Massachusetts Bay Company. These were the Puritans and they, too, came to the New World to find religious and political freedom. The Puritan Fathers had teachings that were strict and stern. They brought with them more wealth than had the Pilgrims, and the colony grew and spread out over New England. Later the Plymouth and the Massachusetts Bay colonies were united.

The design on the stamp is taken from the official seal of the Massachusetts Bay Colony.

Carolina—Charleston Issue of 1930

To commemorate the 250th anniversary of
the founding of Charleston, South Carolina.

The Spanish and the French had attempted to make settlements in Carolina but had failed. It was a group of Englishmen under a royal charter who came to Carolina and in 1680 founded Charles Town, named in honor of the King. A governor of the Carolina Colony and a friendly Indian chief are shown on the stamp. In the border design are a rice plant and a branch of indigo, products which became the most important crops in South Carolina.

Issue of 1930

Following the death of William Howard Taft, a new 4 cent stamp was issued bearing his likeness. This stamp replaced the 4 cent Martha Washington of the current 1922 stamp issue.

A new 1½ cent stamp was brought out with a more satisfactory likeness of Warren Harding. The border design was changed to be uniform with the other stamps of the current 1922 series.
Issued rotary press sheet and coil.

Braddock's Field Issue of 1930

To commemorate the 175th anniversary of the Battle of Braddock's Field in 1755. In connection with the unveiling of a statue of Washington erected at Braddock's Field.

This stamp carries the picture of a statue of young George Washington in the uniform of a British officer. Before the Revolution, General Braddock had been sent to the Colonies to drive the French and Indians from Pennsylvania. The twenty-three-year-old Washington served as Colonel under General Braddock. In the Battle of Braddock's Field the general insisted on keeping his troops in close formation—against the advice of Washington, who already knew the fashion of Indian warfare. In this battle General Braddock's troops were defeated and he himself was killed.

Von Steuben Issue of 1930

To commemorate the 200th anniversary of General Von Steuben's birth in 1730.

Baron Von Steuben, a Prussian with a long training in the Prussian Army, had been aide-de-camp to Frederick the Great. He came to this country during the Revolution and gave invaluable help to America. At Valley Forge he offered his services to General Washington, and there he took over the military training and drilling of the Continental Army. He turned the ragged volunteers into well-trained soldiers. The stamp bears a portrait of Von Steuben.

Pulaski Issue of 1931

In honor of General Pulaski, a hero of the Revolutionary War.

General Pulaski, the son of a Polish nobleman, gave his life for the American cause. He had fought for freedom of his own country until Poland was conquered. Then, coming to America, he joined Washington's army and became a valuable officer. He died during the siege of Savannah. The American and Polish flags are shown back of the portrait of General Pulaski pictured on the stamp.

Red Cross Issue of 1931

To commemorate the 50th anniversary of the founding of the American Red Cross Society.

A Red Cross nurse is pictured on the stamp, which is printed in black with the cross in red.

Through the efforts of Clara Barton the Society of the American Red Cross was established. The wounded and dying soldiers on the battlefields of the Civil War had known the young Clara Barton as she quietly moved among them giving aid wherever possible. Several years after the close of the war, in 1881, the United States officially recognized the Red Cross. Clara Barton became the society's first President. No organization in the world has a greater purpose that the Red Cross—that of giving aid to the suffering in war and in peacetime disasters.

Yorktown Issue of 1931

To commemorate the 150th anniversary of the Surrender of Cornwallis.

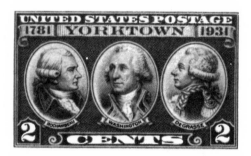

The surrender of General Cornwallis at Yorktown, Virginia, marked the end of the Revolutionary War. The French had come to America's aid. As a portion of the French fleet under Admiral de Grasse moved into Chesapeake Bay, Washington's army and the French troops under General Rochambeau laid siege to Yorktown. There, completely surrounded and cut off from reinforcements, the British general surrendered in 1781.

On the stamp are the portraits of Rochambeau, Washington, and De Grasse. The stamp was printed in two colors.

Washington Bicentennial Issue of 1932

To commemorate the 200th anniversary of the birth of George Washington,
February 22, 1732.

George Washington, "first in war, first in peace, first in the hearts of his countrymen," is alone honored on this issue.

Each stamp carries a different picture of Washington, from a portrait made at some period in his life. The 1½ cent stamp shows him in the uniform he wore as a young colonel of the Virginia Militia. The picture on the 3 cent value shows him as Commander in Chief of the Army, and this portrait was painted during the tragic winter at Valley Forge. The portrait on the 10 cent stamp was painted while Washington was serving his second term as President of the United States.

From a miniature by Charles Wilson Peale painted in 1777

From a bust made by Jean Antoine Houdon in 1785

The "Virginia Colonel" made at Mount Vernon by Peale in 1772

From the Athenaeum portrait painted by Gilbert Stuart in 1796

General Washington painted by Peale at Valley Forge in 1777

From a portrait painted by Peale in 1777

From a portrait painted by Peale in 1795

From a portrait by John Trumbull painted in 1792

From a portrait by John Trumbull painted in 1780

From a drawing from life made in 1798 by Charles B. J. F. Saint Memin

From a drawing from life made in 1795 by W. Williams

From a portrait by Gilbert Stuart painted in 1795

Olympic Winter Games Issue of 1932

*To honor the International Olympic Games held at Lake Placid,
New York, in January, 1932.*

In ancient Greece a national festival of games and chariot races was held on the plain of Olympia in honor of Zeus. The Olympic Games were revived in Athens in 1896. Since then the Olympics have been held at frequent intervals, with athletes from different nations competing.

The third Winter Olympic Games were held in America at Lake Placid. The stamp issued in honor of this event is known as the Lake Placid stamp.

Arbor Day Issue of 1932

*To commemorate the 50th anniversary of Arbor Day
and the 100th anniversary of the founder's birth.*

Arbor Day, dedicated to the planting of trees, is now celebrated as a holiday in many states. Its founder was J. Sterling Morton, a member of the Nebraska State Board of Agriculture, who realized the vital importance to the nation of tree planting. He arranged a contest to see which county in Nebraska, and which person, could plant the most trees in one day. As the result, more than one million trees were planted on the first Arbor Day in that state.

Two children planting a tree are pictured on the stamp.

Olympic Summer Games Issue of 1932

*In honor of the International Olympic Games held at Los Angeles
during the summer of 1932.*

Two stamps were issued at this time. One was of 3 cent denomination, as the letter rate was increased in 1932 from 2 cents to 3 cents an ounce. A modern athlete is shown on the 3 cent stamp, and the picture on the 5 cent value is from an ancient Greek statue called "Discobolus." Discus throwing was one of the main events of the ancient Olympics.

Issue of 1932

After the first-class-mail rate was increased from 2 cents to 3 cents an ounce, this ordinary 3 cent stamp was issued.

The stamp carries the portrait of Washington, conforming to the established policy of having the first President of the United States pictured on the stamp of letter-mail rate. The design is the same as that of the 2 cent Washington Bicentennial stamp, except that the dates under the portrait are omitted.

William Penn Issue of 1932

*To commemorate the 250th anniversary of the arrival
of William Penn in America.*

William Penn was an English Quaker. With the large inheritance left him by his father, he obtained a royal grant to a vast area of land in the New World. In 1698 Penn founded a Quaker colony in the Province of Pennsylvania and laid out Philadelphia. His policy was to live in peace with the Indians and to pay them for their land, and he made a lasting treaty with them.

The stamp shows a portrait of William Penn painted in London when he was twenty-two years old. The numerals indicating the denomination of the stamp are placed on keystones, which are symbols of Pennsylvania—known as the Keystone State.

Daniel Webster Issue of 1932

*To commemorate the 150th anniversary of the birth
of Daniel Webster in 1782.*

Daniel Webster was a New England lawyer and a powerful orator with a gift for words. As a statesman he had great influence in the Senate, where he served for many years and helped to form American policies.

The stamp carries a portrait of Webster with deep-set eyes under shaggy brows.

Georgia Bicentennial Issue of 1933

*Issued to commemorate the 200th anniversary of
the settlement of Georgia by General Oglethorpe.*

At one time in England, people unable to pay their debts were thrown into prison and left there. General Oglethorpe, a Member of the House of Parliament, saw the hardship and cruel injustice of this system. He obtained a grant for a colony in Georgia and, in 1733, brought a group of these unfortunate persons from the debtors' prisons to America. Savannah was the center of the Georgia Colony, which was the last of the British Crown Colonies to be founded in the New World.

The portrait of Oglethorpe shown on the stamp is from a painting made in London.

Peace Commemorative Issue of 1933

*Issued to commemorate the 150th anniversary of the Proclamation of Peace
ending the war for American Independence.*

This stamp, also called the Newburgh stamp, pictures the old stone house in Newburgh, New York, which was Washington's Headquarters during the last years of the Revolutionary War. It was here, in 1783, that General Washington issued to his troops the official Proclamation of Peace marking the end of the American Revolution.

Century of Progress Issue of 1933

Issued to commemorate the Century of Progress International Exposition
held in Chicago in 1933.

In 1933, on Chicago's one hundredth birthday, an International
Exposition was held in that city. Two stamps honoring the event were
issued, a 1 cent and a 3 cent stamp. The 1 cent value shows old Fort
Dearborn, pictured from a replica of the fort which was built on the
Exposition grounds. Fort Dearborn, with its stockaded log fence and its
blockhouse with loopholes for muskets, had been a lonely frontier post
situated where Chicago now stands. In 1812 old Fort Dearborn had
fallen into the hands of the Indians, who massacred the fleeing garrison
and the settlers.

By 1833 Chicago had become just a tiny village. One hundred years
later it was a great city on whose Exposition grounds was erected the
Federal Building, with its modern architecture, shown on the 3 cent stamp.

Souvenir sheets of this issue of stamps were also brought out in honor
of the convention of the American Philatelic Society held in Chicago in
1933. Both designs were issued in sheets of twenty-five stamps each, ungummed and without perforations.

CHICAGO'S FIRST
POST OFFICE 1833

National Recovery Administration Issue of 1933

Issued in the days of depression after World War I to arouse the interest of the nation in the National Recovery Act.

The stamp represents American workers—a farmer, a businessman, an industrial worker, and a woman employee. It is known as the N. R. A. stamp.

Little America Issues of 1933–34

To honor the second Antarctic Expedition and for use on letters mailed through the Little America post office.

At the time of Richard Byrd's second expedition to the South Pole, this special stamp was issued. Covers carrying the stamp and addressed to Little America were forwarded to the Antarctic with a service charge of fifty cents for each letter. The mail was pulled over the snow and ice to a United States post-office tent set up in Little America, the base camp of the expedition. From this post office the canceled mail was sent to New Zealand and from there forwarded to its destination.

The design on the stamp pictures a globe with dotted lines indicating the several flight routes used by Admiral Byrd. Proposed new flights to the Antarctic and to the South Pole are also indicated.

Special souvenir sheets, each containing six Little America stamps, were issued in 1934 to honor the National Stamp Exhibition of New York. These were ungummed and without perforations.

General Kosciusko Issue of 1933

In honor of Thaddeus Kosciusko and to commemorate the 150th anniversary of his admission to United States citizenship.

The picture of the Polish patriot, Thaddeus Kosciusko, shown on the stamp is from a statue in Lafayette Park, Washington, D. C. The Polish general volunteered his services in the American War for Independence. He was a skillful engineer and laid out the fortifications of West Point, then the most important fort on the Hudson River. Kosciusko served throughout the entire war and in appreciation of his services was granted United States citizenship in 1783.

The stamp was of 5 cent denomination, 5 cents being the foreign mail rate.

Maryland Issue of 1934

To commemorate the 300th anniversary of the settlement of Maryland.

The two little sailing vessels pictured on the stamp are the *Ark* and the *Dove*. In 1634 they brought to the New World some two hundred English colonists under Lord Baltimore. The Calvert colonists landed in Chesapeake Bay and founded a Catholic settlement at St. Marys. This was the first Maryland colony. It is the only 3 cent commemorative printed in red.

MARYLAND
COLONISTS

Mother's Day Issue of 1934

A commemorative stamp issued as a tribute to the Mothers of America.

In 1914 Woodrow Wilson proclaimed the second Sunday in May as "Mother's Day." In 1934 this stamp, honoring Mothers, was issued. It carries a design suggested by Franklin D. Roosevelt, adapted from the painting of his mother by James McNeill Whistler.

It was printed rotary press and flat plate.

Wisconsin Territory Issue of 1934

*To commemorate the 300th anniversary of the arrival
of Jean Nicolet in the territory that is now Wisconsin.*

The French trapper and explorer Jean Nicolet was sent to investigate the unknown territory now comprised in the State of Wisconsin. In 1634 he arrived on the shores of Green Bay dressed in silken robes. Nicolet came prepared if, as he hoped, this vast Western land should turn out to be China. Instead of Orientals, Nicolet found only a tribe of Indians with whom he made trade treaties. Several years later the first permanent settlement was made in the Wisconsin territory.

National Parks Issue of 1934–37

*Issued to arouse interest in the National Parks of the
country, 1934 being proclaimed as "National Parks Year."*

This issue was a set of ten large-sized stamps. Each stamp carried a
scene of natural wonder or beauty taken from a different National Park.
The stamps were not issued in denominational sequence.

On the 1 cent stamp is the picture of a great
rocky cliff with perpendicular sides rising more
than three thousand feet into the air. This cliff,
El Capitan, is in Yosemite National Park in California. Indian legend claims that the summit of
the great rock was once the throne of a mighty
chief. The Indian chief forsook his throne to
seek the maiden of a strange tribe who had appeared and then as mysteriously disappeared.
Unsuccessful in his search, he returned to the
valley only to find it forsaken. Climbing to the
top of the cliff, the unhappy chief carved two
faces in the stone—one of himself looking west-
ward in search of the girl and one of a stern-faced warrior who would stand
forever guarding the lands of his people. The faces on El Capitan are still
pointed out to tourists.

The 2 cent stamp pictures the strangely beautiful
rock formations of the vividly colored Grand Canyon in Arizona. Bright Angel Canyon and rocks
formed like oriental temples are shown. Through
many ages the mighty Colorado River has cut
deeper and deeper into the earth, making a great
chasm the bottom of which is a mile below the
original surface. To the American Indian the Grand
Canyon was the home of the Great Spirit and was
forbidden ground.

Mount Rainier National Park in the State of
Washington is honored on the 3 cent stamp. The
high mountain of lava rock, Mount Rainier, was
called "Snow Peak" by the Indians. The summit,
covered with glacial ice, is shown reflected in the
waters of Mirror Lake at its foot.

The apartmentlike homes of prehistoric cliff dwellers are shown on the 4 cent stamp. This Cliff Palace was built in what is now the Mesa Verde National Park of Colorado and here, on the rocky ledge, Indians lived eight centuries ago.

Yellowstone Park, Wyoming, is the largest of our national parks, and in the early days old trappers brought back strange tales of the wonders of this region. The geyser "Old Faithful" is shown on the 5 cent stamp. "Old Faithful" rises into the air about every sixty-six minutes in a 150 foot column of scalding water and steam.

The 6 cent stamp pictures Crater Lake in Crater Lake National Park, Oregon. The lake half fills the shell of an ancient volcano eight thousand feet above sea level. Wizard Island, a volcanic projection within the crater, is shown in the foreground.

On the 7 cent stamp is a picture of "Great Head," a rocky promontory on the coast of Maine in Acadia National Park.

The Great White Throne, on the 8 cent stamp, is in Zion National Park, Utah. It is a strange rock formation, dazzling white at the top, with stratas of red and pink rock at the base.

The 9 cent stamp, featuring Glacier National Park in the State of Montana, shows Mount Rockwell and Two Medicine Lake. On the shores of the lake, Indian legend claims, two mighty medicine men fight for the love of an Indian girl and hurl snow and cold and thunder about the country.

The 10 cent stamp bears a scene of the Great Smoky Mountains in Great Smoky Mountain National Park in Tennessee and North Carolina. These are among the oldest mountains in North America and take their name from a delicate haze that surrounds them.

Souvenir sheets, containing six 3 cent Park stamps, were issued gummed but without perforations in honor of the American Philatelic Society Convention held in Atlantic City in 1934. Later in the same year souvenir sheets with six 1 cent Park stamps, also gummed but without perforation, were issued as a compliment to the Trans-Mississippi Philatelic Exposition held in Omaha, Nebraska.

In compliment to the forty-third annual convention of the Society of Philatelic Americans held at Asheville, N. C., in 1937, the 10 cent stamp was reissued as a souvenir sheet. Here the stamp is printed in blue-green instead of gray, which is its color in the regular issue. It is often called the S. P. A. stamp. Issued gummed and imperf.

Special Printing Issue of 1935

In 1935 a special printing of twenty different commemorative stamps was made to meet the requirements of collectors and the general public. This series is known as "The Farleys." These stamps were obtainable only at the Philatelic Agency in Washington. They were sold in full sheets as printed and in blocks thereof. They were ungummed.

The Proclamation of Peace stamp and the Little America stamp were issued in sheets of 200, flat plate printing, perf. The souvenir sheet of the Little America stamp was issued in sheets of 25 panes of 6 stamps each, flat plate, imperf.

The Mother's Day, the Wisconsin, and the ten National Park stamps were issued in sheets of 200, flat plate, imperf. The souvenir sheets of the 1 cent and 3 cent National Park stamps were issued in sheets of 20 panes of 6 stamps each, flat plate, imperf.

The souvenir sheets of the 1 cent and 3 cent Century of Progress series were in sheets of 9 panes of 25 stamps each, flat plate, imperf.

The 16 cent dark blue Special Delivery Air Mail stamp was issued in sheets of 200, flat plate, imperf.

Connecticut Issue of 1935

To commemorate the 300th anniversary of the settlement of Connecticut.

By 1635 certain dissatisfied colonists of the Massachusetts Bay Colony had moved into the valley of the Connecticut, or "Long River," and settled near Hartford. Sir Edmund Andros, the new Royal Governor sent over from England, arrived at Hartford and demanded that the Connecticut Colony surrender its precious charter to him. The story tells that the box containing the charter was placed in front of him, but suddenly the candles were extinguished and the charter disappeared.

In the hollow of a great oak tree about a mile from Hartford, the charter was found carefully hidden away for safekeeping. Years later the old tree was destroyed in a storm, but the spot where it stood is marked with a monument.

A picture of the old Charter Oak is shown on the stamp.

California Exposition Issue of 1935

*To commemorate the California International Exposition
held at San Diego, California, in 1935.*

This Exposition was held on Point Loma, the tip of land in southern California where the history of the state begins. In 1542 Cabrillo, a Portuguese navigator, had dedicated the land to the Spanish king.

The stamp shows an aerial view of the Exposition grounds with San Diego Bay in the distance. It is known as the San Diego stamp.

The Boulder Dam Issue of 1935

To commemorate the completion of Boulder Dam.

Between the steep rock walls of the Black Canyon the wild Colorado River has been tamed, and is held back by the highest dam ever constructed.

The building of the giant Boulder Dam was a supreme engineering task. It was erected by the federal government to control floods and furnish a vast water supply. The dam is located at a point on the Colorado River boundary line between Nevada and Arizona.

The scene on the stamp represents an aerial view of the canyon, the river, and the construction work of the great dam.

Michigan Centennial Issue of 1935

To commemorate the 100th anniversary of the Statehood of Michigan.

The state seal of Michigan is shown on the stamp with the United States flag and the state flag.

Michigan Territory had been a part of the vast Northwest Territory, known only to explorers and trappers. It had been explored and first settled by the French. Later many settlers began pouring in from the East, and in 1835 the territory applied to Congress for statehood. Because of a boundary dispute it was not until two years later that Michigan was admitted into the Union.

Texas Centennial Issue of 1936

To commemorate the 100th anniversary of Texas Independence.

On the stamp are shown the portraits of Sam Houston and Stephen Austin. The Alamo mission, also pictured, had an important role in the Texas story.

Once a part of the Spanish possessions in America, Texas had passed into the hands of the Mexicans. At that time Mexico offered grants of land in Texas, and Stephen Austin, sometimes called the Father of Texas, founded a settlement of pioneers from the East. More and more farmers and traders streamed into the country, and in 1836 Texas declared her independence from Mexico and war broke out.

The Alamo mission at San Antonio, which had been turned into a fort, was besieged and the Texan heroes defending it were killed to the last man. Later, under the leadership of Sam Houston, the Texans defeated the main force of Mexicans and captured their general, Santa Ana. Texas had won her independence, and became an independent republic.

Rhode Island Issue of 1936

To commemorate the 300th anniversary of the founding of Rhode Island.

The father of the Rhode Island Colony, Roger Williams, is pictured on the stamp. He was a Baptist pastor in Salem, and in 1636 he was expelled from the Massachusetts Bay Colony because he disagreed with its leaders. Roger Williams believed that the government should not force any particular form of religion on anyone. Fleeing to the Narragansett country, he bought land from the Indians—with whom he established friendly relations— and founded Providence, at the head of Narragansett Bay. Rhode Island became a haven of tolerance for the many colonists settling there.

The likeness of Roger Williams shown on the stamp is from a statue in Providence. The state seal appears in the lower left corner of the stamp.

Third International Philatelic Exhibition Issue of 1936

Issued as a souvenir of the Third International Philatelic Exhibition held in Grand Central Palace, New York City, in 1936.

At the time of this exhibition four stamps, each of 3 cent denomination, were reissued together in special sheet form, gummed but without perforations. The four stamps appearing on the sheet were the Connecticut Tercentenary, the California Pacific Exposition, and the Michigan and the Texas Centennial issues. The issue of 1936 is commonly called the "Tipex," signifying the Third International Philatelic Exhibition.

Arkansas Centennial Issue of 1936

To commemorate the 100th anniversary of the admission of Arkansas as a State.

Arkansas was a part of the land included in the Louisiana Purchase and had been first settled by the French. The Old State House in Little Rock is shown on the stamp with the Arkansas Post, captured by Sherman in the Civil War, and the present State Capitol. Arkansas was received into the Union in 1836.

Oregon Territory Centennial Issue of 1936

To commemorate the 100th anniversary of the first white settlers of Oregon Territory.

The central design of the stamp shows a map of the old Oregon Territory, which comprised the present states of Idaho, Oregon, and Washington together with parts of Montana and Wyoming. On the map one historical place in each state is marked, and the first-day sale of the stamp was from each of these five places.

Two missionary families were the first to settle in old Oregon and it was their heroic pioneering efforts that brought the great stream of settlers into the vast territory after 1836.

The old Oregon Trail is outlined on the map. Over this trail the weary wagon trains of the settlers passed, pulled by horses, mules, or oxen. Exhausted and often starving, the settlers, always in danger from Indian attacks, pressed on westward through badlands, past lonely trading posts, and over mountains to frontier homes in the unsettled territory.

Susan B. Anthony Issue of 1936

Issued in honor of Susan B. Anthony in connection with the 16th anniversary of Woman Suffrage.

The American schoolteacher pictured on the stamp spent her long life in reform work. She sought to better the legal standing of women and to obtain for them the voting privilege. She herself insisted on casting her ballot in a state election and was fined for voting without a right, but she refused to pay and the fine was never exacted. In 1920, a few years after her death, the nineteenth amendment was ratified and the women of the United States were granted the right to vote.

Army Issue of 1936–37

Issued in honor of the United States Army.

There are five stamps in this series, in values of from 1 to 5 cents.

The 1 cent stamp carries the portrait of the first Commander in Chief of the Army, General George Washington. Nathanael Greene, a general in the Revolutionary War, is also pictured on the stamp. He was second only to Washington in military skill. Mount Vernon, Washington's home on the Potomac, is shown in the background.

The portraits of Andrew Jackson and Winfield Scott appear on the 2 cent denomination. Jackson, who was known as "Old Hickory," was the general who saved New Orleans in the War of 1812. General Scott captured Mexico City during the dispute over the boundary lines of Texas. On this stamp the Hermitage, the home of Jackson near Nashville, is pictured.

The 3 cent stamp carries the portraits of three Civil War generals—Ulysses Grant, the . Commander in Chief of the Army, William T. Sherman, and Philip Sheridan—who fought on the side of the Union.

Two great generals of the Confederacy—Robert E. Lee, Commander in Chief of the Confederate Army, and "Stonewall" Jackson—are honored on the 4 cent denomination. The birthplace of General Lee, Stratford Hall in Virginia, appears in the center of the stamp.

The National Military Academy at West Point, on the Hudson, is pictured on the 5 cent denomination. Here four years of strict military training are given to cadets selected from each of the states. West Point was a fortified military post during the War for American Independence.

Navy Issue of 1936–37
Issued in honor of the United States Navy.

In the series honoring the Navy there are also five stamps in denominations of from 1 to 5 cents.

On the 1 cent stamp are the portraits of two naval heroes of the Revolutionary War: John Paul Jones, who, with his vessel, the *Bonhomme Richard*, badly crippled, answered the British demand to surrender with the words "Surrender? I have not yet begun to fight," and John Barry, whose first command was the *Lexington* shown on the stamp.

The 2 cent stamp pictures the fearless Stephen Decatur, who brought to an end the reign of the pirates in Tripoli. The other portrait on this stamp is that of Thomas MacDonough, who commanded the *Saratoga*. A small fleet under his command defeated the British in Lake Champlain during the War of 1812.

Admiral Farragut, pictured on the 3 cent stamp, was a naval hero of the Civil War. Lashed to the mast of his flagship, the *Hartford*, he directed the battle of Mobile Bay. The stamp also carries the portrait of David Porter, who aided Farragut in the taking of New Orleans and fought many of the naval battles of the Civil War.

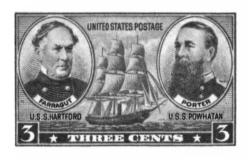

The 4 cent stamp carries the portraits of three of the greatest naval officers in the Spanish-American War. Admiral Dewey, who is pictured in the center of the stamp, destroyed a Spanish fleet in Manila Bay. Under Admiral Sampson and Commodore Schley, our Navy bottled up the Spanish ships in Santiago harbor and then destroyed them as they tried to escape.

The seal of the United States Naval Academy at Annapolis, Maryland, is shown on the 5 cent stamp. At this school are trained chosen men who will become officers in the United States Navy. A cadet of early days and a modern cadet are pictured.

Northwest Ordinance Issue of 1937

To commemorate the 150th anniversary of the Adoption of the Ordinance of 1787.

An ordinance was passed in 1787 which provided for the government of the Northwest Territory and for its division into five parts, each of which would become a state when it had a sufficient number of settlers. Dr. Manasseh Cutler, whose portrait is on the stamp, had much to do with the framing of the ordinance. Rufus Putnam of Massachusetts, also pictured, had been a colonel under Washington and was one of the pioneer settlers in Ohio.

The map on the stamp shows the thirteen original states and the great Northwest Territory, which became the states of Ohio, Indiana, Illinois, Wisconsin, and Michigan.

Virginia Dare Issue of 1937

To commemorate the 350th anniversary of the birth of Virginia Dare and the settlement at Roanoke Island.

This stamp honors the first white child born in America. A group of colonists sent out by Sir Walter Raleigh attempted in 1587 to establish a settlement on Roanoke Island, off the coast of what is now North Carolina.

In the little settlement Virginia Dare was born. She was the grandchild of its governor, John White. Soon after the colony was established the governor sailed back to England for supplies.

Returning to Roanoke Island three years later, he found the fort destroyed and the colonists and his little grandchild gone. The only trace was three letters, C R O, hastily cut in a tree trunk and the word Croatan, the name of an Indian Chief, carved on a fence post.

The Signing of the Constitution Issue of 1937

To commemorate the 150th anniversary of the Signing of the Constitution
of the United States.

In 1787 a group of statesmen gathered at a convention in the State
House of Philadelphia. The fight for independence had been won and a
new nation formed. Now the rules for its government must be made.
George Washington was the president of the meeting. The gray-haired
Benjamin Franklin was a member of the group, as were Alexander
Hamilton and James Madison. After a month of debate the Constitution
of the United States was written, and was signed by thirty-nine men of
faith and courage.

The historic moment of the signing is shown on the stamp.

Territorial Series Issue of 1937

Issued as a tribute to the outlying possessions of the United States.

Four stamps, each of 3 cent denomination, were issued.

The stamp honoring Hawaii pictures King Kamehameha I, who had united the Hawaiian Islands under one rule. The statue of this king stands in Honolulu. American missionaries had gone to Hawaii, and Americans had taken part in the development of the Hawaiian sugar interests. In 1898, at the request of the people of Hawaii, the islands were annexed to the United States and were given a territorial form of government.

Alaska, honored on another stamp of this series, was purchased from Russia in 1867 and, with its fertile soil, its forests and mines, it is the greatest of the outlying United States possessions. Alaska's glacier-capped Mount McKinley, pictured on the stamp, is the loftiest peak on the North American continent.

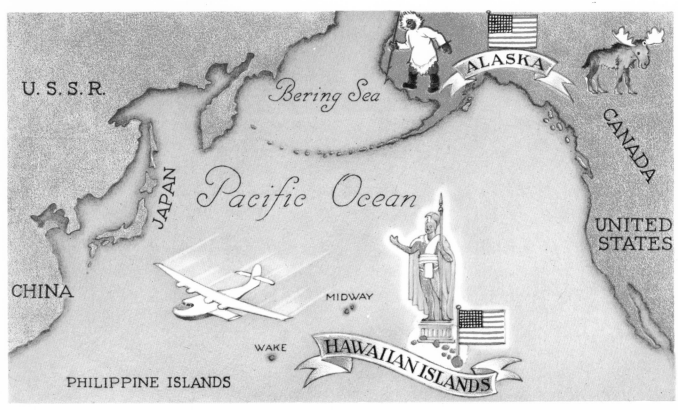

This stamp was issued as a tribute to Puerto Rico, an island in the Caribbean Sea, which was ceded to the United States by Spain after the Spanish-American War in 1898. The stamp pictures the old Governor's Palace known as La Fortaleza.

Close to Puerto Rico lie the Virgin Islands, beautiful tropic islands which now belong to the United States. The Virgin Islands were purchased from Denmark in 1917 as a naval base for Panama Canal defense. The harbor and city of Charlotte Amalie, the capital of the American Virgin group, are pictured on this stamp.

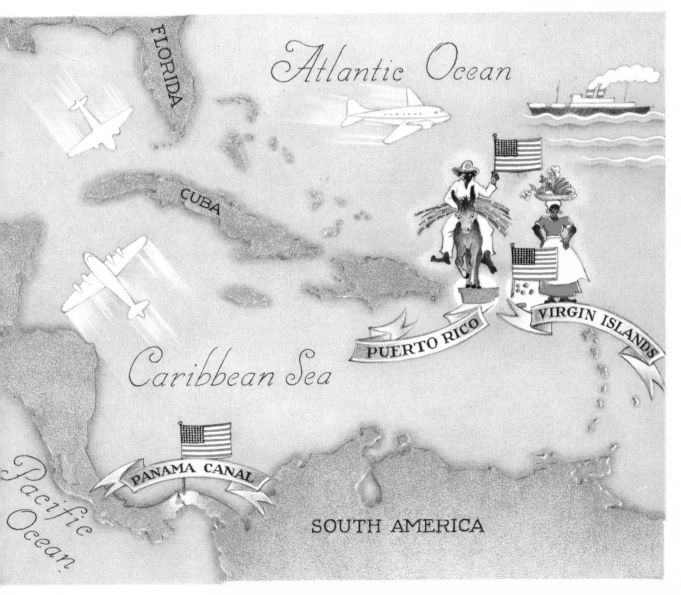

Presidential Issue of *1938*

This regular issue has a simple, uniform design and the stamps carry the portraits of all the United States Presidents from Washington through Coolidge, in the order in which they served. In turn, these Americans have taken the oath of office "to preserve, protect, and defend the Constitution of the United States."

Included in this series are ½, 1½, and 4½ cent denominations which picture Benjamin Franklin, Martha Washington, and the White House.

The $1, $2, and $5 stamps were printed in two colors.

BENJAMIN FRANKLIN

GEORGE WASHINGTON
Served 1789-1797

MARTHA WASHINGTON

JOHN ADAMS
Served 1797-1801

THOMAS JEFFERSON
Served 1801-1809

JAMES MADISON
Served 1809-1817

THE WHITE HOUSE

JAMES MONROE
Served 1817-1825

JOHN QUINCY ADAMS
Served 1825-1829

ANDREW JACKSON
Served 1829-1837

MARTIN VAN BUREN
Served 1837-1841

WILLIAM H. HARRISON
Served 1841

UNITED STATES POSTAGE

JOHN TYLER
1841-1845

10 CENTS 10

JOHN TYLER
Served 1841-1845

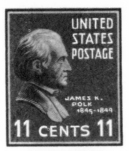

UNITED STATES POSTAGE

JAMES K. POLK
1845-1849

11 CENTS 11

JAMES K. POLK
Served 1845-1849

UNITED STATES POSTAGE

ZACHARY TAYLOR
1849-1850

12 CENTS 12

ZACHARY TAYLOR
Served 1849-1850

UNITED STATES POSTAGE

MILLARD FILLMORE
1850-1853

13 CENTS 13

MILLARD FILLMORE
Served 1850-1853

UNITED STATES POSTAGE

FRANKLIN PIERCE
1853-1857

14 CENTS 14

FRANKLIN PIERCE
Served 1853-1857

UNITED STATES POSTAGE

JAMES BUCHANAN
1857-1861

15 CENTS 15

JAMES BUCHANAN
Served 1857-1861

UNITED STATES POSTAGE

ABRAHAM LINCOLN
1861-1865

16 CENTS 16

ABRAHAM LINCOLN
Served 1861-1865

UNITED STATES POSTAGE

ANDREW JOHNSON
1865-1869

17 CENTS 17

ANDREW JOHNSON
Served 1865-1869

UNITED STATES POSTAGE

ULYSSES S. GRANT
1869-1877

18 CENTS 18

ULYSSES S. GRANT
Served 1869-1877

UNITED STATES POSTAGE

RUTHERFORD B. HAYES
1877-1881

19 CENTS 19

RUTHERFORD B. HAYES
Served 1877-1881

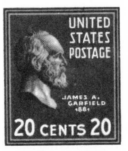

UNITED STATES POSTAGE

JAMES A. GARFIELD
1881

20 CENTS 20

JAMES A. GARFIELD
Served 1881

UNITED STATES POSTAGE

CHESTER A. ARTHUR
1881-1885

21 CENTS 21

CHESTER A. ARTHUR
Served 1881-1885

UNITED STATES POSTAGE

GROVER CLEVELAND
1885-1889
1893-1897

22 CENTS 22

GROVER CLEVELAND
1885-1889, 1893-1897

UNITED STATES POSTAGE

BENJAMIN HARRISON
1889-1893

24 CENTS 24

BENJAMIN HARRISON
Served 1889-1893

UNITED STATES POSTAGE

WILLIAM McKINLEY
1897-1901

25 CENTS 25

WILLIAM McKINLEY
Served 1897-1901

UNITED STATES POSTAGE

THEODORE ROOSEVELT
1901-1909

30 CENTS 30

THEODORE ROOSEVELT
Served 1901-1909

UNITED STATES POSTAGE

WILLIAM HOWARD TAFT
1909-1913

50 CENTS 50

WILLIAM HOWARD TAFT
Served 1909-1913

UNITED STATES POSTAGE

WOODROW WILSON
1913-1921

$1 $1

WOODROW WILSON
Served 1913-1921

UNITED STATES POSTAGE

WARREN G. HARDING
1921-1923

$2 $2

WARREN G. HARDING
Served 1921-1923

UNITED STATES POSTAGE

CALVIN COOLIDGE
1923-1929

$5 $5

CALVIN COOLIDGE
Served 1923-1929

Constitution Ratification Issue of 1938

To commemorate the 150th anniversary of the ratification of the
United States Constitution.

After the Constitution was drawn up and signed at the convention in Philadelphia, it had to be ratified, or approved, by the people. After some delay the approval of nine states was secured and the Constitution became effective.

The stamp pictures horsemen in front of a colonial courthouse, in 1788, hastening to carry forth the news that the Constitution of the United States had been ratified.

On the first-day sale of this stamp in Philadelphia, thirteen stamps were taken from the first sheet printed. One was given to the Governor of Pennsylvania and the rest were sent by homing pigeons to the Governors of each of the other twelve original states of the Union.

Swedish—Finnish Issue of 1938

To commemorate the 300th anniversary of the first settlement
of the Swedes and Finns in America.

In 1638 two ships under the command of Peter Minuit, a Dutch navigator, brought a group of Swedish and Finnish settlers to America. Landing at the Rocks on the Delaware River at what is now Wilmington, they made agreements with the Indians for the purchase of land and built a fort which they named "Fort Christina" in honor of the Queen of Sweden. The settlers built cabins of horizontally laid logs, and this Finnish type of cabin became the pattern for the log house of the American frontiersman.

The scene of the landing is pictured on the stamp.

Northwest Territory Issue of 1938

*To commemorate the 150th anniversary of the settlement
of the Northwest Territory under the Ordinance of 1787.*

The Western wilderness and forests gave way
to the log cabins and clearings of the settlers.
Farmers and traders and miners poured into the
Northwest Territory after the Ordinance of 1787
was passed.

A statue by Gutzon Borglum standing in Marietta, Ohio, was used for the design of this stamp.
It symbolizes the colonization of the West.

Iowa Territory Issue of 1938

To commemorate the 100th anniversary of the establishment of Iowa Territory.

The territory of Iowa was formed from a part of
the vast land included in the Louisiana Purchase.
Père Marquette and Joliet had been the first white
men to visit this section of the country. After Iowa
became a Territory in 1838, thousands of farmers
from New England and other Eastern states staked
out freehold farms and settled there.

The stamp pictures the Old Capitol Building
at Des Moines, Iowa.

Golden Gate International Exposition Issue of 1939

In commemoration of the Golden Gate International Exposition held in San Francisco, California, in 1939.

A large island was dredged from the bottom of San Francisco Bay and here the impressive "Pageant of the Pacific" was held in sight of the Golden Gate. After the close of the Exposition, Treasure Island became one of America's largest airports.

The stamp issued in honor of this Exposition carried a picture of one of the many beautiful buildings, the Tower of the Sun.

New York World's Fair Issue of 1939

In commemoration of the World's Fair opened in New York in 1939.

The World's Fair was held to celebrate the 150th anniversary of the inauguration of George Washington. Engineers and artists turned the marshes and dumps of Flushing Meadows into the vast, beautiful Exposition grounds of the "World of Tomorrow," where fifty-seven foreign countries of the world had buildings or exhibits.

The stamp shows a modernistic treatment of two of the outstanding architectural features of the Fair, the Trylon and the Perisphere.

Washington Inauguration Issue of 1939

To commemorate the inauguration of George Washington as first President of the United States.

After the Constitution of the new nation was ratified, George Washington was unanimously chosen as the first President. The capital of the government was established in New York City. Here, on the balcony of the Federal Building, George Washington, with his hand on the Bible, took the oath of office on April 30, 1789. The cheering crowds gathered below shouted "Long live George Washington, President of the United States," and the guns at the Battery roared their salute.

The inauguration scene is shown on the stamp.

Baseball Centennial Issue of 1939

In connection with the celebration of 100 years of Baseball.

Although colonial boys had thrown off their cocked hats and played an English ball game called "rounders," it is believed that the game of baseball was devised in 1839 by Abner Doubleday, who later became a general in the United States Army. The schoolboys of his time were playing a game with a ball and bat called "One Ole Cat."

Baseball has become America's national game and the stamp pictures boys playing their favorite sport.

Panama Canal Issue of 1939

In commemoration of the 25th anniversary of the opening of the Panama Canal.

In 1550 a Portuguese navigator believed that a passageway could be cut through the narrow isthmus of land connecting North and South America. Through the years, attempts were made by several countries; but all were abandoned.

When Theodore Roosevelt was President, the United States Government took over the gigantic project and built the Panama Canal—a vital link between two oceans. The task was accomplished by Colonel George Washington Goethals, working with a corps of army and navy engineers and doctors. The Canal, with its system of great dams and locks, was officially opened in 1914.

The stamp carries the portraits of Theodore Roosevelt and Colonel Goethals and shows a steamship passing through the Gaillard Cut.

*P*rinting *T*ercentenary *I*ssue of *1939*

To commemorate the 300th anniversary of the
introduction of printing in Colonial America.

The Puritans printed the first book to be made in America.
It was *The Bay Psalm Book*, printed by Stephen Daye in
Cambridge, Massachusetts, in 1640. As a reward the Massachusetts General Court granted him three hundred acres of
land—he "being the first that sett upon printing." The Stephen
Daye Press is pictured on the stamp.

*50*th *A*nniversary of *S*tatehood *I*ssue of *1939*

To commemorate the 50th anniversary of the Statehood of
North Dakota, South Dakota, Montana, and Washington.

By 1889 thousands of settlers had moved into
the great Northern territories of the United States,
and the territories made a plea for statehood. In
the same year North and South Dakota, Montana,
and Washington were admitted into the Union.

A map of these four states is shown on the
stamp. This stamp is jokingly called the "Monday
Wash Day Stamp."

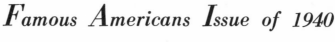

Famous Americans Issue of 1940

Commemorative stamps in honor of famous Authors, Poets, Educators, Scientists, Composers, Artists, and Inventors of America.

In this series there are seven groups of stamps each containing five stamps of from 1 to 10 cent denomination. Portraits of the "Famous Americans" appear on the stamps.

AUTHORS

On the 1 cent stamp is the portrait of Washington Irving, who was one of the very first American storytellers. His tales, such as *Rip Van Winkle* and *The Legend of Sleepy Hollow*, are full of legends and traditions of America.

James Fenimore Cooper, the novelist pictured on the 2 cent stamp, was a master teller of stories of exciting adventure—on the sea, among the Indians, and on the American frontier. The *Leatherstocking Tales* are among his best-known novels.

Ralph Waldo Emerson, shown on the 3 cent denomination, was a New England author and philosopher. In his *Essays* he gave to Americans his great idealistic philosophy.

Louisa May Alcott, whose portrait appears on the stamp of 5 cent denomination, was a teacher and a nurse during the Civil War. She is best known for her book *Little Women*.

The humorist Samuel Clemens, better known as Mark Twain, is shown on the 10 cent stamp. A steamboat pilot on the Mississippi River, a miner and newspaperman, he became one of the great men in American literature. He gave to Americans *Huckleberry Finn* and *Tom Sawyer*.

POETS

Henry Wadsworth Longfellow, pictured on the 1 cent stamp, was a New England poet greatly loved during his lifetime. He was a professor at Harvard University and his life was one of kindliness and generosity. *Evangeline* is one of the many poems he wrote.

John Greenleaf Whittier, whose portrait is on the 2 cent denomination, was of a New England Quaker family and was one of the most loved American poets. In *Snowbound* he gives a family picture of the years he spent on a remote farm. He wrote simple poems such as *The Barefoot Boy*.

James Russell Lowell, shown on the 3 cent stamp, was also a New England poet. He was the United States Minister to England, where he made many friends and won respect for Americans. His poem *The Vision of Sir Launfal* is one of the finest of America's long poems.

Walt Whitman, the traveler poet pictured on the stamp of 5 cent value, was at first condemned because his poetry was so different from the verse which people were accustomed to. Now he is recognized as one of America's greatest poets. The collection called *Leaves of Grass* is one of his best-known works.

James Whitcomb Riley, pictured on the 10 cent stamp, was an Indiana poet who often wrote in the "Hoosier" dialect. His verses are full of pathos and sentiment. He gave us *Little Orphan Annie* and *The Raggedy Man*.

EDUCATORS

The men pictured in this group were untiring in their efforts for educational improvements.

Horace Mann, President of the Massachusetts Senate, was the father of the free American school. He was responsible for a state board of education and secured better schoolhouses. His portrait is shown on the 1 cent stamp.

Mark Hopkins, on the stamp of 2 cent denomination, was also a New Englander. He did a great deal to further the cause of education while serving as President of Williams College for many years.

Charles W. Eliot, whose portrait is on the 3 cent stamp, was a President of Harvard University and there introduced the first written examinations and the system of giving students their choice of subjects.

Frances E. Willard was a teacher and a lecturer and Dean of Women at Northwestern University. She devoted her life to the cause of education and temperance. A portrait of Frances Willard appears on the 5 cent stamp.

Booker T. Washington, who is pictured on the stamp of 10 cent denomination, was born a slave. After a heroic effort to obtain an education for himself, he founded the Tuskegee Institute and devoted his life to the education of the American Negro.

SCIENTISTS

The portrait of John James Audubon, the painter and naturalist, appears on the stamp of 1 cent denomination. Audubon was born April 26, 1785 and was of French descent. He at times made his living as a portrait painter, but his real interest was in birds. He wandered with his notebook and paints throughout the country, studying the birds and the animals of America. He published a volume containing many beautiful color drawings of the *Birds of America*. The Audubon Societies throughout the country are a monument to this great naturalist and artist.

Dr. Crawford W. Long is pictured on the 2 cent stamp. Dr. Long practiced medicine in Georgia and is believed to be the first surgeon to have used ether as an anesthetic in the performance of operations.

Luther Burbank, whose portrait is on the stamp of the 3 cent denomination, was a scientist and horticulturist who developed valuable new forms of plant life. In his experimental farms in California he produced better forms of fruits and vegetables. *How Plants Are Trained to Work for Men* was one of the many scientific books which Burbank wrote.

The 5 cent stamp honors Dr. Walter Reed, the army surgeon who played an important part in the discovery that mosquitoes carry the dread yellow fever. A memorial hospital in Washington, D. C., has been named in his honor.

The portrait of Jane Addams appears on the 10 cent stamp of this group of famous scientists. Jane Addams was a social worker. She was the head of Hull House, the social settlement which did so much for the good of Chicago.

COMPOSERS

Stephen Collins Foster, pictured on the 1 cent stamp, wrote the words and music for many songs of the Old South. His Negro melodies, of which he wrote more than one hundred, are a tribute to his genius. *Old Black Joe* and *Old Folks at Home* are but two of his ballads which have become a part of the tradition of the South.

John Philip Sousa, whose portrait is on the 2 cent stamp, is known as the "March King." He was a bandmaster and composer. Many Americans have marched to the stirring music of his *Washington Post* and *Stars and Stripes Forever*.

Victor Herbert, shown on the 3 cent denomination, is famous for his American light operas. He was born in Dublin, Ireland. During his career he was a cellist, bandmaster, conductor, and composer. *Naughty Marietta* and *Babes in Toyland* are among his many productions which achieved success.

Edward A. MacDowell, whose portrait is shown on the 5 cent denomination, was born in New York City. After studying here and in Europe he settled in New England and devoted himself to teaching and composing. *To a Wild Rose* is one of the compositions for which he is well known.

Ethelbert Nevin, pictured on the 10 cent denomination, was a composer of popular music with sweet melody. He was connected at one time with the music department of Yale University. One of the songs which brought him fame was *The Rosary*.

ARTISTS

On the 1 cent stamp of this group is the portrait of Gilbert Charles Stuart, the American artist whose portraits of George Washington are the accepted likenesses of the Father of his Country. Gilbert painted many of the distinguished men about him and he ranks as one of the great portrait painters of his time.

The portrait of James McNeill Whistler is on the 2 cent stamp. Whistler is famous as a painter and etcher, his etchings ranking with Rembrandt's. He painted many different kinds of subjects and considered color as all-important. The portrait of his mother is one of the world's well-known pictures. An adaptation of this picture was used on the Mother's Day stamp.

Augustus Saint-Gaudens, pictured on the 3 cent stamp of this group, began his career as a cameo cutter. He later became a great sculptor. The statue of General Sherman in Central Park, New York, is one of his best-known works.

Daniel Chester French, appearing on the stamp of 5 cent denomination, was a sculptor famous for his statues of historical figures and for his bas-reliefs. His bronze figure of Abraham Lincoln in the Lincoln Memorial in Washington is a monument not only to Lincoln but to the great genius of the sculptor.

The 10 cent stamp carries the portrait of Frederic Remington, a painter of American Indians and fast-riding cowboys and soldiers of the old Western plains. Remington was also a sculptor and illustrator.

The designs of the 8 and 50 cent stamps of the Trans-Mississippi issue are from paintings by Frederic Remington.

INVENTORS

Eli Whitney, whose portrait is on the 1 cent stamp, was a young New Englander who went to Georgia expecting to teach. On the plantation where he visited he saw the slaves working long weary hours tearing the large black seeds out of each fluffy cotton ball. Deciding that a machine could be made to do this task, he modeled a little cotton gin. Eli Whitney's invention revolutionized the cotton industry.

Samuel F. B. Morse, shown on the 2 cent value, was an artist who tried to support his three children by painting while he struggled to perfect his idea that messages could be sent by electricity. Today Samuel Morse is honored as the inventor of the telegraph.

As a young boy Cyrus H. McCormick, whose portrait is on the 3 cent stamp, worked with his father, who was trying to make a machine which would cut the wheat on their Virginia farm. When he was only twenty-two he discarded his father's ideas, which had failed, and built a machine of his own which, although it was clumsy and rattled about the field, did cut the grain. McCormick improved his reaper and invented and manufactured farm machinery which changed the life of the American farmer.

The 5 cent stamp pictures Elias Howe, who worked in his father's New England textile mills and later in a cotton-machinery factory. The idea of a sewing machine came to him and, after several years spent in developing it, he completed his invention of the lock-stitch sewing machine in 1845.

The inventor of the telephone is pictured on the 10 cent stamp. The Scotchman Alexander Graham Bell came to Boston to teach the deaf to speak. With a knowledge of the functions of speech and with an understanding of electricity, Bell conceived a plan for an instrument which could send the human voice along a wire. He made this instrument and in 1876 was recognized as the inventor of the telephone.

Pony Express Issue of 1940

Issued to commemorate the 80th anniversary of the Pony Express service.

The Pony Express was founded, owned, and operated, without a subsidy, by the great overland freighting firm of Russell, Majors and Waddell, which carried the mail through 2,000 miles of wilderness between St. Joseph, Missouri, and California. St. Joseph was, at the time, the end of the railroad line to the west.

On April 3, 1860, the first daring Pony Express riders started out. One left St. Joseph with mail and headed westward. At the same time another rider raced eastward from Sacramento, California. Relay stations had been established along the wild lonely route—where fresh ponies and riders were in readiness. The first trip was made in each direction in the ten-day time limit. Eighty fearless riders and four hundred fast ponies served the Pony Express during its nineteen months of existence.

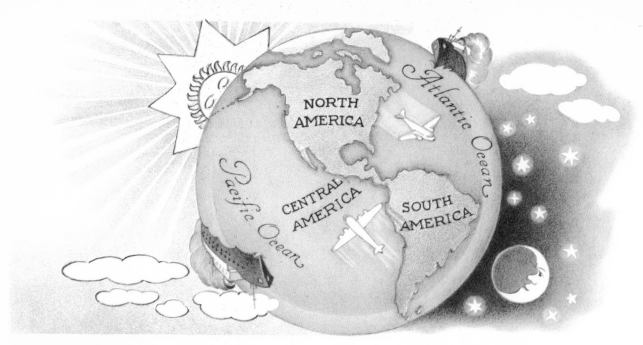

Pan-American Union Issue of 1940

*Issued to commemorate the 50th anniversary of the founding
of the Pan-American Union.*

The Pan-American Union, an organization of twenty-one American Republics, was founded in 1890 to bring the nations of the Western Hemisphere more closely together.

This stamp carries figures from Botticelli's painting of "Spring" and symbolizes friendship between the three Americas—North, Central and South America.

Idaho Statehood Issue of 1940

*Issued to commemorate the 50th anniversary of the admission
of Idaho into the Union.*

Idaho Territory, first settled by the French, became a state in 1890. Its largest city, Boise, was once a small trading post of the Hudson Bay Company. The State Capitol at Boise is pictured on the stamp.

Idaho hunters and trappers, who pushed the frontier steadily westward, were followed by sturdy settlers who cleared the land and built their crude log cabins.

Wyoming Statehood Issue of 1940

Issued to commemorate the 50th anniversary of the admission of Wyoming into the Union.

Many farmers and cattlemen settled on the broad prairies of Wyoming which had been the grazing ground of roaming herds of buffalo. Rich mineral deposits brought miners to the region also.

Wyoming was granted statehood in 1890, the same year in which Idaho was received into the Union.

The stamp pictures the Wyoming state seal with its three figures: a woman, on a pedestal in the center, signifying equal rights, and two men, one representing the livestock and grazing industry of the state and one the mining industry.

Coronado Expedition Issue of 1940

To commemorate the 400th anniversary of the Coronado Expedition through the Southwestern states.

In 1540, while the Spanish conquerors were robbing the Mexicans of their gold and silver, a Spanish explorer, Francisco Coronado, with an armed band of horsemen made his way from Mexico far into the regions west of the Mississippi River in search of gold and other treasure.

Pictured on the stamp are Coronado and his men, the first white men to explore this region.

*N*ational *D*efense *I*ssue *of* 1940

In connection with the National Defense Program.

Three stamps of different denominations, temporarily replacing the same values of the regular series, were issued to call attention to the fact that the security of the United States was in grave danger.

*T*hirteenth *A*mendment *I*ssue *of* 1940

In commemoration of the 75th anniversary of the Thirteenth Amendment to the Constitution.

The thirteenth amendment provided that slavery should not exist in the United States. This amendment was ratified in 1865, a few months after the death of Abraham Lincoln.

The design on the stamp is from a statue by Thomas Ball in Lincoln Park, Washington, D. C.

Vermont Statehood Issue of 1941

To commemorate the 150th anniversary of the admission of Vermont into the Union.

The birthday of Vermont as a state was in 1791. It was the first state to be added to the original thirteen states and is known as the "Fourteenth State."

The State Capitol at Montpelier is shown on the stamp, with a shield containing thirteen purple stars to represent the original states and, above it, a white star representing Vermont.

Kentucky Statehood Issue of 1942

To commemorate the 150th anniversary of the admission of Kentucky into the Union.

The year after Vermont became a state, Kentucky joined the Union. It is now known as the "Blue Grass State." The territory was in the original grant to the Colony of Virginia and was given the name Kentucky, signifying "dark and bloody ground," when it was the scene of Indian warfare.

The daring frontiersman Daniel Boone, pictured on the stamp, blazed the trail and opened the way for settlers.

Win the War Issue of 1942

Issued on July 4th to assert our determination to win the war.

The great eagle with outstretched wings in the form of a V and, encircling it, the thirteen stars of the original states make up the design of the stamp. From Revolutionary days the American eagle, with its great strength and courage, has been the symbol of the American spirit of independence.

Chinese Commemorative Issue of 1942

To honor China and to commemorate the 5th anniversary of the Chinese fight against Japanese aggression.

Abraham Lincoln and Dr. Sun Yat-sen, the founder and the first President of the Chinese Republic, are pictured. These two great men held many beliefs in common. The Chinese characters under Sun Yat-sen's portrait mean "of the people, by the people, for the people" —the words of Lincoln, which also appear under his portrait. The sun with its rays, pictured in the center of the stamp, is the symbol appearing on the flag of China.

CHINA'S GREAT WALL
STARTED 230 B.C.

United Nations Issue of 1943

A commemorative issue to the Nations
United for Victory in World War II.

The stamp pictures an uplifted hand holding the palm leaf of Victory and backed by the uplifted swords of United Nations.

For the first time in history most of the nations of the world combined their military and economic resources and all their energy toward the one objective of winning a war to establish lasting peace.

Four Freedoms Issue of 1943

A commemorative issue to the Four Freedoms.

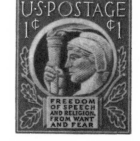

In his message to Congress in 1941 Franklin Delano Roosevelt expressed the principles of the four freedoms which were the aims and hopes of our fighting forces: freedom of speech and expression—everywhere in the world . . . freedom of every person to worship God in his own way—everywhere in the world . . . freedom from want . . . freedom from fear."

The stamp pictures Liberty holding the Torch of Freedom and was designed by Paul Manship.

Overrun Countries Issue of 1943—44

In tribute to the heroic resistance of the countries which
fell under the yoke of the Axis Powers in World War II.

In the series there are thirteen stamps, each of 5 cent denomination. A stamp was issued in tribute to each of the following countries: Poland, Czechoslovakia, Norway, Luxembourg, the Netherlands, Belgium, France, Greece, Yugoslavia, Albania, Austria, Denmark, and Korea.

All the stamps are uniform in border design. At the right appears a kneeling figure; at the left is the Phoenix, symbolizing the renewal of life. This sacred mythological bird was thought to die in a nest of flames and to rise anew out of its own ashes. Each stamp carries the flag of the country honored, and each flag appears in full color in the center of the stamp.

This series was printed by the American Bank Note Company.

UNITED STATES POSTAGE
5 NETHERLANDS 5
CENTS

UNITED STATES POSTAGE
5 BELGIUM 5
CENTS

UNITED STATES POSTAGE
5 FRANCE 5
CENTS

UNITED STATES POSTAGE
5 GREECE 5
CENTS

UNITED STATES POSTAGE
5 YUGOSLAVIA 5
CENTS

UNITED STATES POSTAGE
5 ALBANIA 5
CENTS

UNITED STATES POSTAGE
5 AUSTRIA 5
CENTS

UNITED STATES POSTAGE
5 DENMARK 5
CENTS

UNITED STATES POSTAGE
5 KOREA 5
CENTS

*R*ailroad *I*ssue *of* 1944

To commemorate the 75th anniversary of the completion
of the first railroad across the continent.

In 1869 the tracks of the Union Pacific Railroad, being laid from the East, met that of the Central Pacific, from the West—completing a railway across the United States. The junction was made at Promontory Point, Utah, where an elaborate ceremony was held. Arizona furnished a spike of iron, silver, and gold; Nevada, one of silver. Lastly the gold spike of California was driven into place.

On the stamp is the scene of the Golden Spike Ceremony, from a painting by John McQuarrie.

*S*teamship *I*ssue *of* 1944

To commemorate the 125th anniversary of the first steamship
to cross the Atlantic Ocean.

In 1819 the *Savannah*, a sailing ship with a steam-engine auxiliary, left the port of Savannah and, with sails spread and paddle wheel churning and smoke pouring from her funnel, crossed the Atlantic Ocean. She docked in Liverpool after a trip of twenty-nine days.

The *Savannah* is pictured on the stamp issued in her honor.

Telegraph Issue of 1944

To commemorate the 100th anniversary of the first telegraph message.

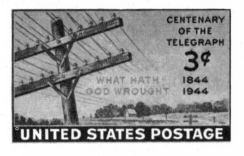

Samuel Morse, an American artist, became convinced that electricity could be used as a means of sending messages instantaneously. Finally he perfected his invention, and in 1844 the first official telegraph message passed over the wires. Anne Ellsworth, a friend of Morse, sent this message, the words of which were "What hath God wrought." Morse, sitting in Washington, tapped out the words. They were received in Baltimore, forty-two miles away, and flashed back to him. A telegraph pole with wires is pictured on the stamp.

Philippine Issue of 1944

Issued in honor of the Philippines.

The stamp shows the fortified island of Corregidor, at the entrance to Manila Bay, and the connecting islands on which were located Fort Drum, Fort Frank, and Fort Hughes, where in 1942 the American and Philippine armies so valiantly resisted the attacking Japanese. Corregidor will always symbolize courage and bravery, and heroism in defeat.

Motion Picture Issue of 1944

To commemorate the 50th anniversary of the Motion Picture Industry.

The design on the stamp, from a photograph taken in the South Pacific, shows members of the American Armed Forces watching a motion picture. The stamp was issued in appreciation of the efforts of the motion-picture industry in the second World War.

Florida Statehood Issue of 1945

To commemorate the 100th anniversary of the admission of Florida into the Union.

Florida, discovered by Ponce de Leon, had in turn belonged to Spain and to England. It was ceded to the United States and in 1845 was admitted into the Union.

The original state seal of Florida is shown on the stamp, with the gates of St. Augustine and the State Capitol at Tallahassee.

United Nations Conference Issue of 1945

To commemorate the United Nations Organization Conference
held in San Francisco.

This stamp, often called the U. N. O. stamp, was approved by President Franklin D. Roosevelt before his death, but had not yet been issued. The words "Toward United Nations" which appear on the stamp, were his and he had fostered the idea of the Conference where United Nations would cooperate in a world organization. When the stamp did come out, his name and the quotation marks had been added.

Armed Forces Issue of 1945

Honoring the Armed Forces of the United States of America.

There are five stamps in this series, each of 3 cent denomination. They were issued to honor the different branches of the armed forces in the second World War and as a tribute to their heroic achievements, which led to victory in 1945.

The first stamp issued was in honor of the Marine Corps. The picture on the stamp shows the raising of the Stars and Stripes on the volcanic summit of Mt. Suribachi during the fearful battle between the attacking "Leathernecks" and the Nipponese. The color of the stamp is the dull green of the winter uniform of the Marine Corps.

The United States Army is honored on a stamp picturing the triumphant "G. I.'s" marching down the Champs Elysées in Paris—with the Arc de Triomphe in the background. These were the fighting sons of the men who, in 1918, had celebrated victory in the same place. The stamp is printed in khaki color.

On the stamp honoring the United States Navy a group of young sailors is pictured. During the second World War the United States Navy, the greatest in the world, covered the seas and destroyed the Japanese fleet. This stamp is printed in blue.

The fourth stamp was issued in honor of the Coast Guard. On the stamp are shown L. C. T. boats heading toward the beaches. One of the many duties performed by the Coast Guard was the delivering of troops to the war-torn beachheads. The color of the stamp is green.

It was the Merchant Marine Corps who, during the war, sustained the ever-extending supply lines so vitally necessary to our Armed Forces and our Allies. The stamp honoring the Merchant Marine Corps pictures a Liberty Ship unloading cargo and is printed in green.

Roosevelt Memorial Issue of 1945-46

In memoriam of Franklin Delano Roosevelt.

Franklin D. Roosevelt, who had served as Assistant to the Secretary of the Navy and as Governor of New York State, came to the White House in 1932, at a critical time in our history. He furthered the ideals of Woodrow Wilson and worked for the good of the people, not only of his own country but of the world.

When the catastrophe of the second World War fell on the United States he summoned together all the resources of the country and inspired the nation's greatest effort toward total victory.

In this series there are four stamps of different denominations; each carries the same portrait of Roosevelt. The 1 cent stamp also shows the library at his home in Hyde Park, his family home on the Hudson.

The "Little White House," the cottage at Warm Springs, Georgia, where the President often went and where he died on April 12, 1945, is shown on the 2 cent stamp.

The 3 cent denomination pictures the White House in Washington. This is the home of the Presidents of the United States while they are in office.

With the portrait on the 5 cent stamp is pictured the globe of the world with the "Four Freedoms" which Roosevelt toiled to secure for all peoples of the world.

Alfred E. Smith Issue of 1945

In tribute to Alfred E. Smith.

Al Smith, the "Happy Warrior" as he was called, served as the Governor of New York State for four terms. The newsboy of New York City, born in humble circumstances, became a man of great influence in the affairs of his state and nation.

Texas Statehood Issue of 1945

To commemorate the 100th anniversary of the Statehood of Texas.

Texas, having gained her independence from Mexico, had become a republic in 1836. In 1845 the "Lone Star Republic" became the "Lone Star State," the largest state of the Union. The star on the flag of the Texas Republic became the twenty-eighth star of the United States flag. This is symbolized on the design of the Texas statehood issue.

Veterans of World War II Issue of 1946

In tribute to the millions of Americans who served in the armed forces of our country during the second World War, this special stamp was issued. The five stars on the stamp honor those who gave their lives in the different branches of the service. The central design of the stamp pictures the honorable-discharge emblem.

Tennessee Statehood Issue of 1946

To commemorate the 150th anniversary of the admission of Tennessee into the Union in 1796.

Tennessee was the sixteenth state to come into the Union. Originally the region, which was an Indian hunting ground, had been a part of North Carolina. The settlers there declared their independence and tried to go their own way as the State of Franklin; but, after being ceded to the Union by Carolina, Tennessee was governed as a territory for a few years. In 1796 it was admitted into the Union as a state.

Two sons of Tennessee are honored on the statehood stamp. The fearless, insistent Andrew Jackson, "Old Hickory" as he is known, broke the Creek warriors and forced them to make peace with the Great White Father in Washington. Jackson proved himself a great general in the War of 1812. He served two terms as President of the United States.

John Sevier, whose portrait is also on the stamp, was one of the pioneers of the Tennessee region. He led the hardy mountaineers against the Indians, who continuously threatened the lives of the settlers. When Tennessee was admitted into the Union, John Sevier was chosen as the first governor of the state. The State Capitol at Nashville is also pictured.

Iowa Statehood Issue of 1946

To commemorate the 100th anniversary of the admission of Iowa to statehood.

Many settlers pushing westward crossed the Mississippi River and laid out farms and built log cabins on the broad prairielands of Iowa Territory, which was a part of the vast lands in the Louisiana Purchase. The territory was called Iowa, meaning "Sleepy Ones," the name of an Indian tribe living in the region. In 1846 Iowa Territory became a state.

The stamp honoring Iowa statehood pictures the flag of Iowa on a silhouette map of the state. The eagle on the flag holds in its beak a scroll with the motto "Our Liberties We Prize and Our Rights We Will Maintain." In the border design of the stamp are stalks of corn. Iowa, the Hawkeye State, is known as "the State where the tall corn grows."

Smithsonian Issue of 1946

To commemorate the 100th anniversary of the establishment
of the Smithsonian Institution at Washington, D. C.

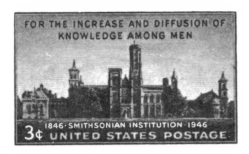

An English scientist, James Smithson, left his entire fortune to the United States Government to be used to establish an American institution of learning. After several years of debate an Act of Congress accepted the endowment and established in 1846 the Smithsonian Institution at Washington, D. C.

The stamp pictures one of the buildings of the Smithsonian Institution and carries the words "For the increase and diffusion of knowledge among men." This quotation is taken from James Smithson's will.

New Mexico Issue of 1946

To commemorate the 100th anniversary of the acquisition of New Mexico.

In 1846, Congress had declared that a state of war existed with Mexico and New Mexico was acquired by the United States. General Stephen W. Kearny led an army of volunteers on a wearisome march of nine hundred miles over the mountains and plains of the Santa Fe trail. On August 18th, 1846 they arrived at Santa Fe which capitulated without a shot being fired. Governor Kearny became the first Military Governor of New Mexico.

The picture on the stamp is from a painting of General Kearny with his troops in front of the Governor's compound in Santa Fe after the flag of the United States had been raised.

New Mexico was first organized as a territory. In 1912, it was granted statehood and became a part of the union of the forty-eight states which now form the United States of America.

Air Mail

The first air-borne letter in the United States was one written by President George Washington in 1793. Jean Pierre Blanchard carried this letter when he rose in a balloon from the Philadelphia Prison yard, with President Washington and others watching the first balloon flight in America. The letter was taken to a town in New Jersey, a few miles distant, where the balloon grounded.

About one hundred years later, on that cold windy day at Kitty Hawk in 1903, the flying machine of the Wright brothers flew for twelve seconds. After that, aviation developed in great strides.

Americans had consistently used the fastest means available for the transportation of mail and, as the flying machine developed, the Post Office Department experimented with the possibility of air mail. In 1911 the first sack of mail was flown by an army pilot from Garden City Estates, Long Island, and delivered at Mineola, a few miles away. Often the experiments in flying mail were made by fearless, reckless, barn-storming pilots in connection with state fairs. These pilots in their flimsy planes carried mail on short-distance hops officially recognized by the Post Office Department, which placed cancellations on the covers carried on these flights. There were no air mail stamps.

This was the pioneering stage of air mail. Regular air mail service was not established in the United States until 1918. By 1946 the United States air mail service extended to all parts of the world.

First Air Mail Issue of 1918

Issued for the air mail service between Washington, Philadelphia, and New York.

In 1918, just before the close of the first World War, Congress finally authorized the Post Office Department to carry mail by plane, and the first official air mail route lay between the cities of Washington, Philadelphia, and New York. At this time there were but few civilian pilots and it was the War Department which furnished the planes and pilots for the service. The planes were discarded training planes and most of the pilots were army pilots released from the services.

The first official air mail stamp was of 24 cent denomination. It carried a picture of a "Jenny," one of the Curtiss planes used to carry the mail. The stamp was printed in two colors.

In this first issue a sheet of 100 stamps which was sold at a Washington post office contained one of the greatest rarities to be found in air mail stamps. The airplanes on this sheet appeared inverted in the frames.

Twenty-four cents an ounce was the required air mail rate and this included special delivery service. Two months after the 24 cent stamp was issued the rate was reduced to 16 cents and a second air mail stamp, of 16 cent denomination, appeared. In the same year a 6 cent stamp was issued when the air mail rate became only 6 cents an ounce. However, the 6 cent stamp did not include special delivery. Both the 16 and the 6 cent stamps were of the same design as the 24 cent denomination but were printed in only one color.

Air Mail Issue of 1923

Issued for use in the transcontinental air mail service.

It was soon realized that carrying mail by air for short distances saved but little time. Air mail routes were extended section by section and by 1920 they reached from coast to coast.

Mail planes had flown only in the daytime and the bag of mail had been transferred to trains at night, with other fliers picking it up and carrying it on in the morning. Experiments were made in flying by night, and by 1924 night-flying service was established. Every twenty-five miles along the mail route revolving beacon lights were set up, and their powerful rays swept the sky and guided the pilots. Planes were equipped with emergency flares that could be dropped by parachute to help locate a field in case of forced landing. But it was a lonely, dangerous job for the pioneering night-flying pilots in their open-cockpit planes. In spite of the many crack-ups and forced landings these pilots mapped the skyways and flew the mail continuously across the continent.

The mail route to the West was in three zones: New York to Chicago, Chicago to Cheyenne, and Cheyenne to San Francisco. The rate for each zone was 8 cents an ounce.

Three new air mail stamps were issued for this service. One was of 8 cent denomination and carried a design of the radiator and propeller of a mail plane. The 16 cent stamp showed the official insignia of the air force. On the 24 cent stamp of the series was the picture of a De Haviland mail plane, which now took the place of the "Jenny" and traveled with a top speed of one hundred and twenty miles an hour instead of the Jenny's ninety miles an hour.

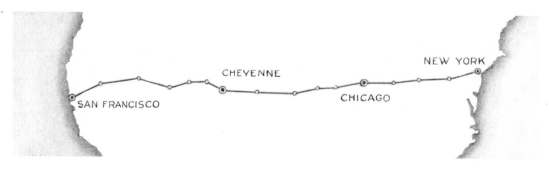

Map Air Mail Issue of 1926-27

Issued to meet the new rate of air mail postage.

By 1925 the government air lines were well established; but to encourage civil aviation Congress adopted the plan of letting commercial companies fly the mail, and contracts were given out. The first contractor ready to fly was the Ford Motor Company.

Many new connecting air lines were established and air mail service spread quickly over the United States.

The new rate of 10 cents for each ounce of contract air mail made it necessary to issue a 10 cent air mail stamp. This stamp was of larger size, to avoid confusion in the post office between the regular stamps and the air mail stamps. The design on the stamp shows a map of the United States and two mail planes, one flying to the East and one flying westward.

A little later the 15 cent stamp of this series was brought out, followed the next year by a 20 cent stamp issued when the air mail rate became 10 cents for each half ounce regardless of distance. As most letters weighed more than one-half ounce, a 20 cent value was necessary. The three stamps of the series carried the same design.

Lindbergh Issue of 1927

*To honor Colonel Charles A. Lindbergh and the first nonstop flight
from New York to Paris.*

At dawn in the fog and the misty rain of a May morning in 1927, a young air mail pilot took off from the soggy runway at Roosevelt Field, New York. In his plane *The Spirit of Saint Louis*, a monoplane with Whirlwind motor, he headed up the coast and then out over the north Atlantic. His plans had been carefully made, and his equipment checked. This was the first attempt of any airman to cross the Atlantic alone.

Thirty-three and one-half hours later the plane dropped out of the night above Le Bourget Field near Paris . . . circling low over the field, it landed. Captain Charles Lindbergh had made the first nonstop flight between New York and Paris. The news of this flight thrilled the world.

In honor of Lindbergh an air mail stamp of 10 cent denomination was issued bearing a picture of his plane, *The Spirit of Saint Louis*, in flight across the Atlantic. This stamp temporarily displaced the current 10 cent air mail stamp of the 1926 issue.

The Lindbergh stamp was also issued in booklet form.

Beacon Issue of 1928

Issued to meet the new 5 cent air mail rate.

After Lindbergh's flight, interest in aviation and in air mail increased. It was possible to reduce the air mail rate to 5 cents for the first ounce and 10 cents for each additional ounce. The new stamp of 5 cent denomination was issued in a large size and was printed in two colors. It carried a picture of the great beacon light on Sherman Hill in the Rocky Mountains.

This stamp proved very costly to manufacture and two years later a a new air mail stamp took its place.

Winged Globe Issues of 1930–34

Issued to replace the 5 cent Beacon issue.

The new 5 cent stamp was printed in only one color. It carried the design of the insignia of an air mail pilot, the globe with extended wings. The stamp was first printed flat plate and in 1931 was printed by rotary press to further reduce the manufacturing cost.

In 1932 a stamp of 8 cent denomination with the same design was brought out when the air mail rate was increased to 8 cents for the first ounce.

In 1934 the rate was reduced to 6 cents an ounce and a stamp of 6 cent denomination with the same design was issued.

The darkest period in the story of United States air mail came in 1934, when the Government cancelled all civilian air mail contracts and the Army Air Corps took over the task of flying the air mail. It was in the winter, the most dangerous flying time, and, while the pilots had the necessary courage and daring, they had neither the training nor the equipment for air mail flying. One army airman after another crashed and was killed. After six months the government turned back the air mail service to civilian contractors.

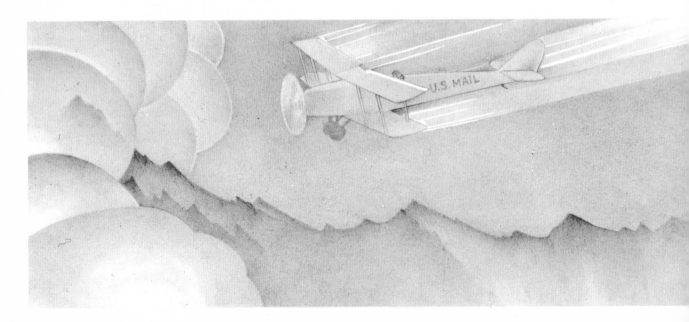

Graf Zeppelin Issue of 1930

Issued for use on mail to be carried on the European-Pan-American round-trip flight of the Graf Zeppelin.

The giant airship *Graf Zeppelin* made the first airship flight around the world. The following year, when the *Graf Zeppelin* was planning a round-trip flight from Germany to the United States by way of Spain and South America, the Postmaster General decided, as a gesture of good will, to issue a series of stamps to be used on cards and letters carried on this flight.

Three special air mail stamps were issued. The 65 cent stamp pictures the *Graf Zeppelin* in flight across the Atlantic in an eastward direction. The $1.30 value shows the airship flying westward between the continents, and the $2.60 stamp pictures the airship in front of the globe. The different denominations cover the rates to and from the various points touched by the *Graf Zeppelin* on this round trip from Friedrichshafen.

Century of Progress—Graf Zeppelin Issue of 1933

Issued for use on mail to be carried on the special flight of the Graf Zeppelin to the Century of Progress Exposition.

When the World's Fair, the "Century of Progress," was held in Chicago in 1933, the *Graf Zeppelin* made a special flight to this Exposition. The great airship left Friedrichshafen and proceeded to Chicago by way of South America. She stopped at Miami and Akron for refueling before going on to Chicago. The Post Office Department issued a stamp of 50 cent denomination to be used on United States mail which would be carried on the airship from Miami and Akron for delivery within the United States and from Miami, Akron, and Chicago for dispatch to Europe on the return trip.

The design of the stamp shows the *Graf Zeppelin* in flight. The hangar at Friedrichshafen is pictured at the right side of the stamp and the Federal Building of the Century of Progress Exposition at the left side.

Trans-Pacific Issues of 1935–37

Issued for use on mail carried by the Trans-Pacific air mail service.

In November, 1935, the gleaming giant *China Clipper* took off from Alameda Airport, California, for the first round-trip flight to Manila by way of Honolulu, Midway, Wake, and Guam. The flight of this sky pioneer of the Pacific, with its load of mail, marked the beginning of commercial air service across the Pacific Ocean.

For mail carried by the Trans-Pacific service an air mail stamp of 25 cent denomination was issued, primarily for air mail to Hawaii, Guam, and the Philippine Islands. The stamp pictures the *China Clipper* in flight over the Pacific far above a Chinese junk, a sailing ship, an old-type steamship, and a modern liner. The shield of the United States and the shield of the Philippine Islands are also shown on the stamp, which carries the date of the *China Clipper's* first flight across the Pacific.

After the Trans-Pacific service proved successful, the route of the Clippers was extended to China and to Macao in the China Sea. The rates were lowered in 1937 and two new air mail stamps were issued—of 20 and 50 cent denomination. These were of the same design as the 25 cent stamp but without the date, which had appeared on that stamp.

Eagle and Shield Issue of 1938

Issued in connection with National Air Mail Week celebration.

As the use of air mail increased, it was felt that a new, distinctive stamp for the regular 6 cent rate was needed. At the suggestion of Franklin D. Roosevelt the American eagle and shield were used in the design of the new stamp, and it was printed in two colors.

Trans-Atlantic Issue of 1939

Issued in connection with the inauguration of Trans-Atlantic air mail service.

On May 20, 1939, the *Yankee Clipper* of the Pan-American Airways took off from Port Washington, Long Island, and arrived in Lisbon, Portugal, twenty-six and one-half hours later. This was the first scheduled trip of the Trans-Atlantic service.

For the air mail crossing the Atlantic, a new 30 cent stamp was issued. The stamp bore the design of the winged globe similar to the regular air mail issue of 1930. The words "Trans-Atlantic" were added and the background of the design was changed slightly.

Twin-Motored Transport Issues of 1941—44

Issued for use on all air mail services of the United States.

A series of stamps of different denominations, all similar in design and printed in beautiful colors, was issued for all United States air mail flown to all corners of the earth. The design pictures a twin-motored transport in flight.

There are seven stamps in the series, in denominations of 6, 8, 10, 15, 20, 30, and 50 cent, all issued in 1941 except the 8 cent which came out in 1944.

The 6 cent stamp was also printed in booklet form.

Air Mail Issue of 1946

To meet decrease in the Air Mail postage rate

Effective October 1, 1946, the air mail postage rate was reduced to 5 cents an ounce for mail sent between all points in the United States and its possessions, Canada, Mexico and to members of the armed forces abroad. To provide for the reduced rate a 5 cent air mail stamp was issued on September 25, 1946.

The design on the stamp is of a four-engined Douglas transport plane in flight.

On the day on which the 5 cent rate became effective, two transports were temporarily converted into "flying mail cars" and crossed the continent one from the Atlantic and one from the Pacific coasts. Letters carried on the "flying mail cars" were sorted and cancelled by mail clerks during the flight.

Air Mail Special–Delivery Issue of 1934–36

Issued to give combined air mail and special delivery service in one stamp. The 6 cent air mail postage rate was combined with the 10 cent rate for special delivery and in 1934 a new 16 cent air mail stamp came out. The stamp carries the picture of the Great Seal of the United States, a design suggested by Franklin D. Roosevelt.

In 1935 the "Farley" special printing of this stamp was issued.

In 1936 this same stamp was reissued in two colors to make it more distinctive and to avoid confusion for postal clerks.

Special Delivery

Issues of 1885 and 1888

So that certain letters could reach their destination more quickly than by regular mail, Congress instituted a special delivery service in 1885. A 10 cent stamp was issued which when added to the regular postage assured immediate delivery from a special delivery office or from offices serving places with a population of more than four thousand. The stamp pictured a running messenger boy and carried the words "Secures immediate delivery at a special delivery office."

The special delivery service was improved when, in 1888, a new 10 cent stamp was issued which was good at any post office and could be used on a package as well as on a letter. This stamp was of the same design as the first special delivery stamp, but the wording was changed to read "Secures immediate delivery at any post office."

The Columbian Exposition Issue of 1893

The color of the 1888 issue was changed from blue to orange in 1893, at the time the Columbian commemoratives were issued. This was done to avoid confusion between the 1 and 4 cent Columbians, which were similar in color to the blue special delivery stamp. The orange color was used for about one year. In 1894 the stamp was again printed in blue. A line was added under the words "Ten Cents."

Issues of 1902–1917

Bicycles came into use in the postal department and a new special delivery stamp was issued carrying the picture of the messenger boy on a bicycle instead of on foot.

The issues of this stamp have different perforations and are with and without watermarks, as this design was in use for twenty years.

Issue of 1908

A special delivery stamp of a new shape and new design was issued in 1908. This stamp pictures an olive branch and the winged hat of Mercury, the fleet messenger of the gods. It is often called the "Merry Widow" issue. As it was not a distinctive enough stamp for special delivery, it was discontinued after a year and the old design of 1902 reissued.

Issue of 1922

The fast motorcycle took the place of the bicycle and a special delivery stamp was issued with the design of a carrier and his motorcycle.

Printed flat and rotary.

Issue of 1925

Special delivery service came to be more widely used both for packages and for letters; so two special delivery stamps of new denominations were issued, a 15 and a 20 cent value. The 15 cent stamp was of the same design as the 10 cent 1922 issue. The 20 cent denomination carried a new design of a motor truck and a carrier loading special delivery packages.

Printed flat and rotary.

Issue of 1944

The rate for special delivery mail was increased in 1944 and two new denominations of stamps for this service were issued during the year, a 13 and a 17 cent stamp. The design on both of these stamps is identical to that of the 1922 issue—picturing the carrier and his motorcycle, with only the values and the color changed.

Issues of 1925–28

A special handling stamp of 25 cent denomination was issued in 1925. Later, in 1928, there was added a 10, a 15, and a 20 cent denomination with the same design. The special handling stamps used on fourth-class mail matter secure the same handling given to first-class mail matter.

Parcel Post

In 1912 a set of twelve special parcel post stamps were issued. These were for use on only parcel post packages. However, in 1913 the Postmaster General directed that regular postage stamps could be used on parcels and also that the parcel post stamps were valid for all purposes for which regular stamps were valid.

The parcel post stamps were in use until the supply was exhausted, but after the first printing no further printings were made.

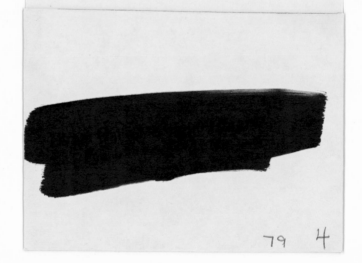